A Son of the
QUEEN CITY

A Son of the
QUEEN CITY

Cincinnati Memories

Richard L. Grupenhoff

Copyright 2023 by Richard L. Grupenhoff

All rights reserved.

Published in the United States of America by:
Dr. Richard L. Grupenhoff
Sewell, NJ

ISBN: 979-8-218-36537-0

Editor/cover design & photos—Carol Ann DeSimine
Book Interior and E-book Design by Amit Dey | amitdey2528@gmail.com

This book is protected by copyright. No portion of this book may be used or reproduced in any manner whatsoever, electronic or mechanical, including on websites and social media, without the written permission of the author, except in the case of brief quotations embodied in critical articles and reviews.

ACKNOWLEDGEMENTS

I wish to thank all those who have supported and encouraged me to complete this work. I would not have finished it without you. I also want to thank all those who have provided much of the historical information that serves as a background for this book. They include the archivists and fact checkers at the Cincinnati Public Library, the Cincinnati Historical Museum, the Archdiocese of Cincinnati, Saint Aloysius Orphanage of Cincinnati, and the Franciscan Friars at the Province of Saint John the Baptist.

DEDICATION

This book contains a brief record of my family's history, and for that reason I dedicate it to our ancestors, upon whose shoulders we have built our lives. This book also contains my recollections of Cincinnati and the neighborhood of South Fairmount, where I was born and raised. I dedicate it to the memory of that part of South Fairmount that was once there but now no longer exists.

I also dedicate this album of memories to my loved ones: my partner, Carol Ann DeSimine; my sons, Richard and James; to my siblings and relatives, and to my grandchildren, their children, and the generations to come.

No one is ever free until they tell the truth about themselves and the life into which they have been cast. Write it down, tell it to a friend in need.... We are all here to be a witness to something, to be of some aid and direction to other people.

~ Tennessee Williams

CONTENTS

Prologue xiii
1. Remembering 1
2. Awakening. 5
3. The Queen City 9
4. Roots 17
5. My Parents 25
6. Saint Bonnies 35
7. South Fairmount 65
8. Invisible Boy. 75
9. Shadwell Park 83
10. My Life With The Boogie Man .89
11. The Sailboat 97
12. My Life In The Movies 101
13. Death By Algebra 113
14. My Life With William Shakespeare 117
15. Mary White 127

16. Joseph Hendker 131

17. Life Lessons 135

18. Three Years Before The Mast 143

19. As Luck Would Have It 169

20. College Days. 171

21. JFK'S Funeral 183

22. Lorenzo Tucker 187

23. The End Game 197

Epilogue 199

About the Author 201

PROLOGUE

This is how this book came to be: in 1998 I received an email from a university student in Germany. She wrote that her grandmother's maiden name was Grupenhoff, and that her grandmother was apparently the last of that name still living in Germany. They had searched the internet databases and all the German phonebooks and found that there were no more Grupenhoffs listed anywhere in Germany, and they wanted to know about the descendants of those Grupenhoffs who emigrated to America in the 1800s.

At the time I was in my mid-50s, and while I'd previously made some tentative explorations into my family's history, I'd discovered very little. My siblings and I only knew the names of our grandparents, and that was as far back as we could go. For a long time we felt that was as far as we would ever go. But this email also revealed that there was a farmhouse just outside of Osnabrück named "Hof Grupenhof." It belonged to the family for 300 years, and we were invited to come visit and reconnect with our old-world relatives. I accepted the invitation and traveled to Osnabrück in the summer of 1999.

It was a decision that changed my life. Before the visit I'd considered myself orphaned from my past, but when I went to Germany my relatives revealed to me a family tree that went back ten generations to the early 1700s. Discovering my family's history was like discovering a whole new world, and I decided to find out as much as I could about my ancestors. One of the first things I learned while searching for my family roots is that I owe so much to my ancestors, who overcame great difficulties while emigrating to America. They often endured much suffering and experienced many disappointments. At the same time, they struggled to provide sustenance and opportunities for the advancement of their children and grandchildren. The simple truth is that we are only here because of our ancestors.

If we were to take time and examine closely the palm of our hand, we would come to realize that our hand contains millions of cells and bits of DNA information we have received from all those relatives who have gone before us. Part of them remain alive inside us, and it is the combination of those bits of their DNA that make us look the way we do: the color of our hair, our eyes, our skin. And I am also convinced that not only do we inherit physical traits from them, but we also inherit some of our ancestors' behavioral traits as well, emotional traits that have some influence on the way we feel and act today.

Soon after I began my research I came to understand that even though I was exploring the lives of my grandparents and great-grandparents and beyond, I was actually discovering who I was, and why I was born of my parents, and why I was born in Cincinnati Ohio, and why I lived the first seventeen years of my life in the neighborhood of South Fairmount, and why I attended Saint Bonaventure Church and grade school, and, finally, why I became who I had become. That was when I decided to write this record of my memories.

When I first began jotting down these memories I assumed I would only be able to fill a few pages or so, because I couldn't remember much of my childhood. My past seemed merely gray, cloudy, and uneventful. Nevertheless, I began writing and, to my astonishment, the more I wrote, more and more memories would bubble up from my unconscious and demand to be recognized and recorded. Many of them found their way into this book.

To place these memories in their proper perspective, I've also included short informal histories of my native city, my neighborhood, and my church and education. Although these memories might not always agree with how Cincinnati, South Fairmount and Saint Bonnies might be remembered by others, I have tried to record the facts and feelings of my life as honestly as I could. And if my memories bring to mind memories of your own, then I will have achieved one of the goals I had when I began this book. I hope you enjoy reading it as much as I enjoyed writing it.

Richard L. Grupenhoff
Sewell, New Jersey
September 2, 2023

1

REMEMBERING

Memory is the treasury and guardian of all things.

~ Cicero

Memory is essential to our understanding of the world and our place in it. At the dawn of civilization, before writing was invented, oral tradition was the main method of memorizing and transmitting knowledge from generation to generation, and if one generation failed to transmit its knowledge to the next, all its collective tribal wisdom would fade into the past, forgotten and irretrievable. But once writing was invented, mankind could store these memories on stone and clay tablets, then on parchment, papyrus, paper and, eventually, in books and digital media. Once these memories were recorded, they could then be retrieved whenever they were desired.

And so it is today. Books and digital media are our treasuries that contain the past memories of our civilization. Without these past memories to build upon, life would be indeed chaotic, if not impossible. We would have to reinvent the wheel every day. In fact, a large part of the intellectual and artistic history of Western Civilization in the thousand years between the fall of Rome and the rise of the Renaissance is the story of recovering the written texts of the Greek, Roman, Islamic and Judaic classics that had previously been lost. These records and memories continue to serve as the foundation of our civilized world to this day.

We are alarmed by stories of libraries and art works deliberately being damaged and destroyed to suit someone's religious or political ideology. And the fire that almost completely destroyed Notre Dame Cathedral in Paris in 2019 surprised and saddened us because we instinctively realized that this great church, part of the collective memory of humanity for over eight hundred years, was almost entirely erased by fire in less than a day.

That's why, when someone's house burns down, the thing they most want to save from the fire is the family photo album, the key that unlocks their library of visual memories and stories of the important people, places and events of their lives. What Cicero meant when he said that memory was the guardian of all things was that memory treasures the experiences of the past and guards them from being lost to us forever.

The same holds true with our individual lives. To a certain degree we are all our own personal historians, defining our past and present through the memories we retain and recall. Who we are is constructed by the genes we've inherited from our ancestors, by the environment in which we were born and live, by the choices we make, and by the random chances and the unpredictable accidents and events that, at times, impinge upon our lives and change them dramatically.

Some suggest that by telling our personal stories we become the stories we tell about ourselves. In effect, we create—and are daily creating—who we are. So, there's no need to spend our lives asking the age-old question, "Who am I?" There is no "who you really are" out there, floating around in space. You are who you are, right here, right now, reading this sentence, and you are the sum total of your life up to this moment.

We create who we are on a daily basis through every choice and decision we make, day-by-day, hour-by-hour, moment-by-moment. We are, with every breath, the very person we have been looking for, our identities constructed by our past experiences that helped to shape who we are now in this present moment. We stand in this "Now," this present moment, with one foot in the past and the other on the threshold of the future, the still-to-come Tomorrowland that we try to shape and influence with our plans, hopes and dreams.

Yet, while we make plans for tomorrow, we have no ultimate control over them. We may "wish upon a star," but chance may intervene, and unforeseen events and accidents might occur that alter those wishes and plans. We can only wait for the future to arrive before we'll know for sure what it will reveal, and whether or not our plans and goals have been realized. As Cincinnati native Doris Kappelhof (Doris Day) once sang, "*Que sera, sera*" ("Whatever will be, will be").

Our very humanity begins with our memories. Without our memories we have no sense of self, no identity. And, by definition, without an identity we're nobody. Anyone who has observed a victim of dementia slowly lose his memory and slip into a state of infancy can attest to that. It is a heartbreaking experience to watch someone forget how to do simple things like getting dressed, to forget the faces and names of those whom they have previously loved and held close, and even to forget how to speak and eat. In the end—and worst of all—they forget who they are. In losing their memory they've lost their selves, their personhood, their very identity.

Like many people my age, I sometimes wonder if I too might someday succumb to this debilitating disease, when my "senior moments" become more than simple forgetfulness. That's part of the reason I decided to recall and record my memories here and now in my 82nd year, to put them into words that will serve as a testimony to my identity and my place and time in this world. Granted, it's not always easy to remember things about one's past, especially as one grows older, but I find myself compelled to record these few brief memories of my life, if only to help me understand who I have become.

My personal philosophy is that the purpose of life is, simply, to live it as best one can, which is both the easiest and hardest thing to do. As Seneca pointed out two thousand years ago, "Learning how to live takes a whole life, and it takes a whole life to learn how to die." While I never achieved great fame or fortune, I am pleased to report that I was nevertheless able to achieve some meaningful success and happiness and a sense of satisfaction with my life. I consider myself one of the lucky ones, especially when I reflect upon how much chance and circumstance have had an impact on me. When I was young I didn't plan much of my future. It just... happened. Still, I believe that chance and circumstance, along with the unconscious urges that simmered up inside me, often seemed to steer me in a certain direction and influence me in making decisions that eventually helped shape my life.

I also believe that this world, here and now, is the only Heaven I'll ever know, so I am trying to enjoy it the best I can, realizing that this life of mine will not last. Death's footsteps get louder every month, so I'm doing all my remembering now and recording what I can. I don't pretend that all the memories I list here are 100 percent factual in every detail. We all know that memory sometimes has a strange way of manipulating and reshaping past events. But I must insist that the memories recorded here are emotionally factual, for they detail how I felt about what I did and what was done to me at the time it was happening.

What follows are the memories of a son of the Queen City.

2

AWAKENING

*There is always one moment in childhood
when the door opens and lets the future in.*

The Power and the Glory
~ Graham Greene

I remember exactly the day my conscious life began, the day when that door opened and let my future in. It was my fourth birthday, Sunday, September 2, 1945, the day of my earliest memory. Granted, I had a few vague memories before then, but they were merely images that flashed before me like still photographs, shadowy vestiges of events that began to trigger my budding self-awareness. They contained little context and less meaning. But my fourth birthday was the first day that provided me with a memory complete in a narrative form that I vividly recall, and on that day for the first time I became aware of the world around me and my place in it.

It was early morning when I came downstairs from my bedroom in my pajamas and bare feet and entered the kitchen. The first to greet me was our new dog, Poochie, a playful little puppy who immediately proceeded to welcome me by licking my toes. It tickled and was funny at first, but soon Poochie started nipping at my feet and ankles. I'm sure he meant no harm, but what started as play soon became painful. To escape him I climbed up on a kitchen chair. Poochie continued to attack me, but he wasn't big enough to jump onto the chair. I was alone and trapped, and I started crying and calling for Mom.

Mom was in the living room when she heard my cries, and she hurried to the kitchen. She grabbed Poochie by the collar and ushered him into the next room and shut the door, and then came back and sat down in the chair next to me. She then reached over and took me into her lap and embraced me. Consoling me, she said, "Richard, you are so lucky!"

"Why?" I asked, brushing the tears from my eyes.

"Because today's your birthday, and guess what? The Japanese have surrendered today, and the war is over!"

She hugged me real tight and kissed me on the cheek and said, "I love you!"

Mom was obviously very happy that the war was over, and that it happened on my birthday. But, at four years old, I had no idea that there was a war going on, or even what war was. My mother had not only delivered me into this world of the living four years earlier, but at this moment she also ushered me into the world of memory and experience, thereby opening the door and letting my future in.

Having Mom hug me and tell me that she loved me was the warmest and happiest I can remember being at that age, and I'm sure that that highly charged emotional moment was the reason I remember the incident so clearly. It was so wonderful to be embraced, kissed, and told that I was loved. I could have thrived on more of the same.

Unfortunately, very little of that happened again for quite a long time. Thirty-seven years later, in May 1982, we were at Saint Bonaventure's auditorium for the celebration of the 50th anniversary of my parents' wedding. I asked Mom to dance, and once we were on the dance floor we joined together for a slow tune. For the first minute or two we danced and said little to each other. But then, she looked up to me and smiled and said, "I love you."

"I love you, too, Mom," I replied, and we danced to the music in a warm and joyful silence.

There they were, almost four decades apart, the only two times I can now recall that my mother ever told me that she loved me. My father, on the other hand, never told me once. Still, that dance was a warm and gratifying moment for me, and I cherish its memory. Later in life I came to realize that both my parents loved me, although they didn't express it physically or vocally. Instead, they exhibited their love by their acts of caring, feeding and clothing me, and by their desire to give me, and all six of their children, as safe and pleasant an existence as they could provide.

Wedding photo of Lawrence Grupenhoff and Alvina Hesselbrock, 1932.

3

THE QUEEN CITY

And this song of the vine
This greeting of mine
The winds and the birds shall deliver
To the Queen of the West
In her garlands dressed
On the banks of the Beautiful River.

Catawba Wine
~ H.W. Longfellow

Written in 1854, Longfellow's poem helped spread Cincinnati's fame during the 1850s. By that time many luminaries of the age, including former President John Quincy Adams, the Marquis de Lafayette, Charles Dickens and Walt Whitman had already visited the city. Dickens described Cincinnati as "A beautiful city; cheerful, thriving and animated." Years before Longfellow wrote his famous poem, Cincinnati had already been called, as early as 1819, "The Queen City" and "The Queen of the West." There were a number of other references as well. For example, In 1844 an early German travel writer, Friedrich Gerstäcker, wrote, "Cincinnati, the Queen of the West, the El Dorado of the

German emigrant! Ask a German who is traveling into the interior from one of the seaports, where are you going? And the answer will invariably be – 'to Cincinnati.'"

Originally named Losantiville by one of the surveyors who laid out the settlement in the late 1780s, the village's name was changed to Cincinnati in 1790 by General Arthur St. Clair, the first governor of the newly designated Northwest Territory. St. Clair renamed the village in honor of the Society of the Cincinnati, a group composed of former officers who served in the Revolutionary War. The society, in turn, was named after the Roman military general, Cincinnatus, who lived around 500 BCE. Tradition has it that after quelling a rebellion he rejected the position of dictator of Rome and instead returned home to tend to his farm. For that reason, he is recognized as a model of public service and civic virtue.

Cincinnati had already become a thriving frontier town of about 800 inhabitants by the time Ohio achieved statehood in 1803. It was the first American city founded west of the Alleghenies after the Revolutionary War and, for fifty years, from around 1810 to 1860, it was a boomtown. By 1829 the town had mushroomed to over 9,000 people. Strategically located on the Ohio River and snuggled in the lowlands surrounded by seven hills, pre-Civil War Cincinnati grew to be the sixth largest city in the United States by 1830, and it became the agricultural, industrial and artistic hub of America's expansion westward.

Prior to 1830 Cincinnati was populated primarily by American settlers from the East Coast. Many of them were New Jersey veterans of the Revolutionary War who had been given land grants as payment for their military service. Around 1830, however, many of the new settlers were immigrants who began arriving from Europe, especially from Germany and Ireland.

In the 1830s land and shipping agents began posting advertisements throughout Germany. *"Alles Spreche von Nord Amerika"* ("All the talk is about North America") was the rallying cry of these agents who sought to entice people in Germany to come to America. Land was cheap and jobs were plentiful, they proclaimed. Many Germans, especially the poor who had little hope for advancement in Germany, responded, hoping to start a new life in the New World. My German ancestors were among those who answered this call, and they became part of the large German migration to Cincinnati in the mid-1800s.

By 1850 Cincinnati's population had increased to 115,000 residents, of which 33,000 were immigrants from Germany. Their presence essentially helped to transform Cincinnati into a German city in the heartland of the United States. The 1910 census revealed that out of a total population of 363,000, more than 125,000 people—over one-third of the city's total population—indicated that the German language was their mother tongue.

From the mid-1800s and into the 1900s the majority of German immigrants lived in a twelve-block section in the northern part of the city. With streets named after German writers like Goethe and Schiller, and after the city of Bremen, this area came to be known as the *"Uber dem Rhein"* ("Over-the-Rhine") neighborhood—the Rhine in this case being the Miami-Erie Canal, built between 1825 and 1845. It traversed the center of the city on its way from the Ohio River to Lake Erie. The canal through Cincinnati no longer exists, having been filled in to create Central Parkway, but the neighborhood is still called the "Over-the-Rhine" district, and today it remains one of the largest urban historic districts in the United States.

By the middle of the nineteenth century both public and parochial school systems had instituted bi-lingual education programs, with courses being taught in both English and German. There were a large number of German-language newspapers during this time, and some of them had circulations over 10,000 by 1900. At least one of these newspapers was Jewish, for by 1900 there were nearly 15,000 German Jews living in Cincinnati.

This flowering of German culture in middle America was unique. Many German immigrants also settled in St. Louis and Milwaukee, and the three cities formed what was once known as "The German Triangle." The German influence might have continued to the present day had it not been for the world wars. Unfortunately, Cincinnati's German American culture was one of the major victims of World War I. When the United States entered the war against Germany in April 1917 there was a crackdown in Cincinnati against anything and everything German. Shortly after the war began "pink slip day" occurred, as "Hun-tongue" teachers were fired from schools, and the entire German collection of the Cincinnati Public Library was hidden away in the library's sub-basement. Streets had their German names erased and were renamed. Some people were attacked and beaten for speaking German in public.

In 1919, after the end of the war, Prohibition became the law of the land. Most believe this law was the result of pressure from morality groups like the Women's Christian Temperance Union, which influenced Congress to pass the 18th Amendment, prohibiting the selling and consumption of alcoholic spirits. But others have suggested that the law was also passed to destroy the German American brewing industry, thereby erasing the most basic of German American social gathering places, the saloons and biergartens. As a result, if there remained disgruntled Germans who were unhappy with the outcome of the war, they would not be able to meet in the biergartens to plot further actions against the American government.

While some German customs may have lingered on during the 1920s and '30s, World War II against Nazi Germany was the second blow to the German influence in the city. Consequently, in the 30-year period from 1915 to 1945, the once-thriving German culture that helped define the character of Cincinnati had been almost completely erased. However, in the past few decades the German presence in Cincinnati has undergone something of a renaissance, and German groups and societies and their celebrations have been revived. Today, for example, Cincinnati boasts that it is home to the largest Oktoberfest in America.

* * * * *

Having been born in Cincinnati, I am a native son of the Queen City. But I also have a unique second claim to this title, for not only was I born **in** the Queen City, but I was also born **at** 1805 Queen City Avenue on September 2, 1941, in the neighborhood of South Fairmount. Directly across the street from my birthplace was Saint Bonaventure's Roman Catholic Church, which was to have a significant impact on my early moral and intellectual development.

My parents were hard-working, quiet and pious folks, rarely given to emotional displays, although my fondest memories of them are of those occasions when they were both laughing. They talked very little about the past, and they didn't make a big fuss about our ethnic background. I was not conscious of this while I was growing up, but I have since come to understand why it was the case.

First, most immigrant families from Europe, while retaining some of the customs of the old country, desired to become part of American culture and reap the benefits of assimilation. One of the reasons they came was that America was the new land of opportunity, and it provided them a chance to start a new life. My ancestors were no different. Secondly, there was something else that hastened their assimilation into American culture, something that practically forced them to abandon many of the traditions and customs of their ancestors. That "something else" were the two world wars. As a result, many German American families sought to distance themselves from their mother country out of fear of punishment and retribution from the non-German majority.

Growing up in America just after the World War II with a name like Grupenhoff was not the best of circumstances. German Americans were obviously not the most popular ethnic group at the time, although I wasn't aware of any prejudice against us, since many of the people in my neighborhood were of German heritage as well. We lived in a neighborhood that was an enclosed urban village where everyone more or less knew everyone else, thought the same and worshipped the same. We were neither ostracized nor persecuted by one another. But our understanding of our situation, even if it were in some cases only intuited, was that it was important to keep a "low profile," to shroud our past in silence, and to purge ourselves of our cultural heritage as much as possible so we would be considered Americans, not German Americans. In short, we had to assimilate in order to avoid discrimination and retaliation.

For example, my father told me that his older brother, my Uncle Frank, had to change his last name from Grupenhoff to Grayson just after WW I in order to keep his managerial job with the Red Cross. When my father told me this story I had a vague feeling that my uncle had betrayed his family and his past. Still, I could understand his predicament and commiserate with him.

If there was any prejudice directed towards me in those days just after the war, it was also the result of my name. Some people had a hard time pronouncing it and spelling it (in fact, still do), and they often laughed at it derisively. As a result, I grew up somewhat ashamed of my last name and, by extension, the German heritage that had given me that name. While I would not change it, I would rather it not be spoken, and it always made me self-conscious when I had to introduce myself. Happily, I no longer have such feelings.

My mother told me that when she started grade school at Saint Bonaventure's around 1915 the nuns were teaching German as well as English, but when the United States entered the World War I in 1917, the teaching of German was prohibited. That was why, my mother ruefully explained, she had never learned German properly, though she did retain a few words and phrases she learned from her parents that she carried with her for the rest of her life.

So, there I was, growing up in Cincinnati in the 1940s in a family and a neighborhood and a city that was essentially encouraged to forget its history and customs. Rather than being celebrated, traditional German customs were eradicated. We were, essentially, separated from our past, orphans from our own history.

That didn't matter much to me as a young boy, however, since I wasn't really aware of what was happening in the larger social and political arenas beyond my neighborhood anyway. Besides, I always thought of myself as an American only, not German American, a phrase I never heard used to describe us in those days, and it's still rarely used today. As a result of this purging, the German culture my parents and grandparents had experienced had all but disappeared by the time I was five years old. In a sense, I had no ethnic past. All I knew then was that I was an American, and I grew up fiercely loyal to my country and the city of my birth.

4

ROOTS

*To forget one's ancestors
is to be a book without a source,
a tree without roots.*

~ Chinese Proverb

Even though we look to the future, we nevertheless remain products of the past. Our ancestors helped to define who we are, just as we help to define who our children, grandchildren and great-grandchildren will be. It's important to remember one's ancestors and to try to discover who they were, in order to be part of a family tree with roots. Also, in the act of exploring and documenting the lives of our ancestors we find that we are actually discovering ourselves. We learn not only who we are, but also why we are here—right here, right now.

Everyone has a story to tell. Unfortunately, my siblings and I were told very few stories about our ancestors. It seems as if my parents remembered little or nothing of what their parents told them, or if they did, they didn't pass any information on to their children. We were a family without memories. Why this was the case, we shall never know. When America joined the world war in 1917, my father was nine and my mother was seven. Because of the suppression of all things German, they might have been immediately cut off from exploring or discussing their family's past, since practically no stories about our ancestors have been passed down orally.

Of course, there are official records, such as birth and death certificates, records of marriages, ship manifests and census lists. I have sifted through many of these records off and on over the years as I worked on reconstructing my family tree. Aside from these records, however, there were almost no personal stories handed down through my family's generations, stories of how and where someone grew up, what kind of job they had, what emotions they felt, what they believed in, and what significant events shaped their lives. This lack of information is one of the reasons I set out to record and restore what little there was of my family's history.

Both of my paternal great-grandparents, Franz Grupenhoff (1843-1877) and Katherina Wissing (1846-1928), came from northwestern Germany. The same is true of my maternal great-grandparents, Herman T. Hesselbrock (1842-1919), and Caroline Burrichter (1847-1914). All four of my great-grandparents sailed to America between the years 1850-1870, and their families can be traced back three hundred years to their roots in and around Osnabrück, a city that was then part of the Kingdom of Hanover, but it is now part of the state of Niedersachsen (Lower Saxony), in northwestern Germany.

My paternal great-grandparents came to Cincinnati in the middle of the 1800s, and they are the progenitors of my line of the Grupenhoff family in America. What little we know about Franz is revealed only through four official documents. First, there is a record of his birth in Osnabrück in 1843. Second, when Franz was 21, he arrived in Baltimore by ship from Bremerhaven in 1864 at the height of the Civil War, and immediately traveled to Cincinnati. Third, six years later, in 1870, he married Katherina Wissing. Fourth and finally, Franz died in July of 1877 at age 34, a victim of cholera.

We know little of his life during the thirteen years he lived in Cincinnati, except that he was a day laborer and at times a wagon driver for one of the many breweries in the city. Other than that, there are no stories that have been handed down through the family about his personal life.

We know from official records that Franz existed, but we have no idea who he was. There are no records of his hopes and dreams, how he related to his wife and children, what he enjoyed or disliked. Were he and Katherina in the large crowd that day in 1871 when the Tyler-Davidson Fountain, "The Genius of Water," was brought from Germany and unveiled in the downtown center of Cincinnati on Fifth Street? And how did his wife nurse him in those last agonizing days of his life? Was she by his side, holding his hand as he passed away? Were his children in the room, gathered around him for the last time, not really comprehending what was happening? These things we'll never know and can only imagine, since there are no family stories about what happened in those days.

Mary Katherina Grupenhoff (nee Wissing) 1846-1928.

Marie Katherina Wissing's story is more complex than her husband's, and even more disheartening. She was born in Heek, Germany in 1846, to Bernard Wissing (1810-1853) and Marie Adelheid Hoelscher (1812-1883), my great-great-grandparents. The family set off for America, the land of promise, in 1853, when Katherina was only seven years old. She left from Bremerhaven with her father, mother and three younger siblings on a ship called "New England." While they set out with high hopes, the voyage they took turned out to be one of the worst passages in the history of 19th Century immigration.

We can only imagine what it must have been like during those weeks at sea. Immigrants were cramped below decks in steerage, the cheapest of accommodations. The ship was overcrowded, ventilation was limited, food and water were inadequate and often denied to the passengers. Sanitary conditions were intolerable. Dysentery and sea sickness caused many to die at sea.

The Wissing family was hit particularly hard, as Bernard, the father, and the three younger children were all stricken with illnesses and died at sea, where they were buried. None of them would ever have the chance to experience America. Of the four hundred emigrants on that voyage, more than one hundred died at sea. Of the Wissing family, only Katherina and her mother, Marie Adelheid, survived the passage, and they arrived in New Orleans on December 27, 1853.

Immediately after their arrival, the German passengers sued the captain of the ship to make restitution for their suffering and losses. However, six months later, in June 1854, the New Orleans courts ruled that the captain was innocent of the charges and blamed the German passengers for their own miseries and misfortunes.

It is difficult to comprehend the anguish and anger the survivors suffered on this trip. Add to that the personal grief and suffering Marie

Adelheid and seven-year-old Katherina underwent as a result of losing four members of their family. It must have been very difficult for them to continue their journey, but they had no other choice. So, Marie Adelheid decided that she and her daughter would push on, joining the other German immigrants who were also headed to Cincinnati.

Already by 1853 there were many steamboats plying the Mississippi River, so it's safe to assume that the German immigrants booked passage on a steamboat that would take them up the Mississippi River, and then up the Ohio River to Cincinnati, a trip that lasted another six to eight weeks in the middle of winter. It was undoubtedly a somber and grief-filled journey for Marie and Katherina, both now alone and essentially stranded in this foreign country, unable to speak the language. Many tears must have been shed for their lost ones as they traveled to their new home. All the dreams and hopes their family had when they left Germany were now shattered. The only consolation and assistance they might have received came from the other German passengers who were traveling with them to Cincinnati.

The next evidence we have of Katherina is from 1870, where it is recorded that she was married in Cincinnati, at 24, to Franz Grupenhoff. Over the next seven years the couple had four children: Henry August (my grandfather), William Christian, Frank and Clara. Henry August married Anna Vornhagen in 1898.

Unfortunately, Katherina was to suffer another loss that echoed her earlier one. On July 2, 1877, Franz died a lingering and painful death from cholera. His death at the young age of 34 left his widowed wife destitute, with little means of support for her and the four children. Katherina, now 31, found it necessary to appeal to Catholic charities for help, and she placed her two oldest sons, Henry (now six), and William (now five), in Saint Aloysius Orphanage.

Like her mother before her, Katherina also lost her husband, and she was now separated from her two oldest sons. Six years later, in 1883, her mother, Marie Adelheid, also passed away. These traumatic family deaths and separations must have resulted in much psychological pain for Katherina and her children, and her struggle to continue under such adverse conditions can only be viewed as heroic.

We know little more about her, except that by 1890 her two sons, whom she had placed in the orphanage, had been released and were living with her again, where they remained until they married and moved away. Katherina died in Cincinnati on February 20, 1928, at the age of 81, and was buried in Calvary Cemetery in Evanston, Ohio. Her grandson, my father, undoubtedly knew her, since he was 20 years old when she died, yet he never once told his children anything about his grandmother.

Of my mother's grandparents we know even less. Born in a small village just outside of Osnabrück Germany, Herman Theodor Hesselbrock (1842-1919) came to America with his parents in 1860. His future wife, Caroline Burrichter (1847-1914) was born in Beesten, Germany, and also came to America around 1860. They were married in Cincinnati in 1865 and settled in South Fairmount, where Herman's father, Gerhard, started a dairy business on Selim Avenue.

One of their sons, Henry Herman Hesselbrock (1868-1940), married Maria Anna Hindricksen (1871-1945) in 1898. They had seven children, the last being my mother, Alvina. My maternal grandfather, Herman, as he was called, lived his entire life on Selim Avenue, much of which was spent overseeing the dairy business that his father had left him. He retired from that business in 1925, and later worked as a custodian at Saint Bonaventure's church and school. Anna continued to live at 2212 Selim Avenue until her death in 1945.

An informal wedding reception, probably in Burnett Woods, for Henry Grupenhoff (upper right with black hat and coat) and Anna Vornhagen (in white, next to him), 1898.

Wedding photo of Henry Grupenhoff and Anna Vornhagen, 1898.

Wedding photo of Herman Hesselbrock and Maria Anna Hindricksen, 1898.

5

MY PARENTS

Children begin by loving their parents;
as they grow older they judge them;
sometimes they forgive them.

The Picture of Dorian Gray
~ Oscar Wilde

I was the third son and fourth of six children (Paul, John, Roseann, Richard, Claire and Joyce) born to Lawrence and Alvina Grupenhoff. My father, Lawrence (1908-1983), was the son of Henry and Anna Grupenhoff, my paternal grandparents. My mother, Alvina (1910-1983), was the daughter of Herman and Anna Hesselbrock, my maternal grandparents.

My father, Lawrence William Grupenhoff, was born on West Liberty Street in Cincinnati on June 8, 1908. He was the fourth and final child born to Henry and Anna Grupenhoff. Dad grew up in the "Over the Rhine" section of Cincinnati, yet he told his children next to nothing of his childhood, not even where he went to elementary school. He did mention that he went to high school until his sophomore year, when he was forced to leave because his family needed him to go to work and

Grupenhoff family photo, 1956. Rear, from left: Richard, Paul, Lawrence, Alvina, John, Roseann. Front: Claire, Joyce.

contribute to the family's income. He married Alvina Marie Hesselbrock in Saint Bonaventure's church on May 28, 1932. By the time I was born in 1941, my family was living in an apartment at 1805 Queen City Avenue.

One day when I was about eight, my older brother John took me downtown to visit Dad where he worked at Goodrich Tire & Rubber Company on Court and Race Streets. Before that visit I really didn't know what Dad did for a living, and when we walked into his office we found him talking on the telephone with his feet up on his desk. I remember that I was very impressed by the fact that he had his own office and desk. He then showed us around the other areas of the business, but there was nothing much to look at except piles of tires and more tires, and the whole building was filled with the smell of rubber. I thought that if there were a fire the place would burn for days.

Dad explained that it was his job to keep track of the tires coming in and going out, counting them and filling out a daily inventory report. He was, essentially, a "numbers cruncher," a clerk in a position between management and the blue-collar laborers who loaded and unloaded the tires. He wore a white shirt and tie to work every day, as he and his older brothers were the first generation to move up from the laboring class. Dad could probably tell you everything there was to know about tires, like the meaning of those model and psi numbers molded on the side of them.

Dad also took me to a number of Cincinnati Reds baseball games. We would walk across the lower level of the Western Hills Viaduct down to Spring Grove Avenue and then south to Western Avenue, where Crosley Field was located. I remember one night game we attended around 1948 or 1949, when the Brooklyn Dodgers and their new star, Jackie Robinson, were in town.

We sat in the cheap seats in the upper deck down the right field line at Crosley Field, surrounded by a sea of black faces, all of whom cheered Robinson every time he came up to bat, and every time he made a good play in the field. I thought their behavior was strange, since the fans were from Cincinnati and should have been rooting for the Reds. But then again, after reading about Jackie Robinson in the newspaper, I too wanted him to do well, for I was glad that he had broken the color barrier, and that the only thing that mattered now on the baseball field was not the color of your skin, but how well you performed between the foul lines.

Why I was so aware of race relations at such a young age I can only attribute to my father's influence. Dad was a New-Deal Democrat who turned twenty-one the year the Stock Market crashed. He voted a straight Democratic ticket for presidents from FDR through JFK to Jimmy Carter. He supported the working class, unions and civil rights. He was also active in community politics and was a member of the South Fairmount Improvement Association, where for a while he served as its president.

In 1953 my friend Alan Hammann and I decided to save our money from our newspaper jobs to buy tickets for the All-Star Game that was to be played in Cincinnati in July. My father and Alan's accompanied us. We sat in the right-field bleachers at Crosley Field and watched as our hometown heroes, Ted Kluszewski and Gus Bell, started the game.

We also saw many future Hall of Famers that day, including Stan "The Man" Musial, Roy Campanella, Mickey Mantle, Joe DiMaggio, Yogi Berra, "Pee-Wee" Reese, Richie Ashburn, Robin Roberts, Warren Spahn, Eddie Matthews and Enos Slaughter, who made a remarkable sliding catch directly in front of us in right field. And we also saw the great Satchel Paige, who by this time was well over 40, pitch an inning or two. Ted Williams, who was not in uniform because he had just returned from flying Sabre Jets in Korea, threw out the ceremonial first pitch. When the game was over Cincinnati fans went home happy because the National League won, 5-1.

On hot summer nights Dad would take his gallon jug down to Ernie Hammann's Cafe and buy a half-gallon of Hudepohl draft beer and bring it home and sit out on the back porch, where he would drink his beer and smoke an Ibold cigar while listening to the Reds' baseball game on the radio. The announcer was Waite Hoyt, the former Yankee pitcher and Hall-of-Famer. Now and then I would sit outside with Dad after I had come home from playing with my friends, and one night when I was about ten years old I joined him, listening to the game between the Reds and the Pittsburgh Pirates being played in Pittsburgh.

Between innings I mentioned to Dad that I thought Waite Hoyt had a great job because he was able to travel from city to city with the team to watch and broadcast the games on the radio.

"What are you talking about?" Dad said. "Waite Hoyt doesn't travel with the team. He's in a radio studio downtown, sitting next to a ticker tape machine that reports the play-by-play of the game in Pittsburgh."

At first I couldn't believe it, but these were the days before TV and big money in baseball, and the teams didn't have the budgets to send their broadcasters along with the players when they travelled to other cities. Yet Waite was so good at providing a colorful commentary that he made you feel that he was right there at the game. If he received a ticker-tape message saying that a player had just flied out to left field, he would boost tension by exclaiming, "There's a ball hit to left field, and Jimmy Greengrass is going back, back to the wall... and... he *makes* the catch!"

During rain delays, Waite would fill the time by regaling his radio listeners with humorous stories about his days with the Yankees and his former roommate, Babe Ruth, who was apparently quite a character both on and off the field. I enjoyed listening to these stories almost as much as I enjoyed listening to the game.

My mother, Alvina Hesselbrock, was born at 2212 Selim Avenue in South Fairmount on September 13, 1910. Like her father, Herman, she lived her entire life in South Fairmount. During her first fifteen years she undoubtedly helped out tending her parent's dairy farm, although she told her children nothing about those days. The 1930 census listed her working as a secretary when she was just nineteen. In 1931 she met Larry Grupenhoff, and they were married in the middle of the Great Depression on May 28, 1932.

Like most mothers in those days, Mom was the glue that held our family together. While Dad would leave home every day to go to work, Mom tended to their children and the household. She cooked, ironed, shopped for groceries, washed the laundry—all those chores that came with raising a family. And they were difficult chores, indeed.

Imagine it's a Monday morning in November 1948. Alvina, now 38 years old and mother of five, rises from her bed at 6:30 a.m. to prepare breakfast for her husband Larry, who has just gone down to the basement to shovel coal into the furnace and relight the fire that had gone out during the night. The house has grown cold, and the temperature is in the upper 40s, so Mom turns on all four of the burners on the stove top to help heat up the kitchen while the children remain warm in bed, still asleep beneath their featherbed quilts.

Mom fries up the first batch of goetta and scrambled eggs for Dad so he can leave the house by 7:15 to catch the #9 John Street trolly at the bottom of the hill to get to work downtown by 8 a.m. A mixture of shredded pork shoulder, pin-head oatmeal and spices, goetta was a northwestern German peasant dish Mom learned from her mother. Many housewives of German descent in Cincinnati made goetta, and it has since become a signature dish of Cincinnati.

Once Dad leaves, Mom fries up a second batch of goetta and also makes a pot of oatmeal for the kids, who must be off to morning Mass and school by 7:40. Once the kids are out the door Mom sits down for her breakfast and a cup of coffee. Then she dresses in her boots and overcoat and ties a scarf around her head and picks up her wicker basket filled with dirty clothes and lugs it outside and down into the freezing basement and begins to wash the laundry.

Her old, dilapidated washing machine barely operates anymore, but she fills it with water and tosses in the first batch of clothes. Later, after the clothes are washed and rinsed, she wrings them out through the hand-cranked rollers on top of the machine. When each batch is finished she drops it into the basket and takes it outside, but only after she has loaded the next set of dirty clothes into the washing machine.

The air is brisk and raw, and her fingers grow numb as she hangs the wet clothes on the line, fastening them with clothespins, one piece after another. The clothesline sags from the weight of the wet clothing, and she stops now and then to pick up a wooden pole of about six feet long with a notch at the end to engage the line and boost it up so the clothes will not drag across the ground. For the next three hours she continues this cold, backbreaking work of washing and hanging the laundry of the entire family, which now consists of seven people.

Mom performed this weekly job for almost forty years without fail, and every Tuesday she would iron the clothes she washed the day before. Yet I never heard her complain, and she rarely missed a Monday in the basement, except for those times when she was having another baby. I don't remember her ever being sick in bed, unable to do her chores. Still, I must confess that when I was young I never really appreciated her labor, and neither I nor my siblings ever gave her credit for her contributions. We were mostly only concerned about ourselves and getting through the day. But these days I remember her warmly and thank her silently every time I go to my basement to do my laundry in my modern washer and dryer—a much easier job than she ever had.

Mom was not the best cook, but she was a good one, and she worked hard to put healthy and tasty food on the table. While we had large meals on all the holidays, they were not the most memorable. Our most ethnic German meals took place on Saturday afternoons in late spring when we worked outside digging up the backyard and planting the vegetable garden.

For lunch on those Saturdays Mom would prepare a buffet table that included pickled pigs' feet, sauerkraut, baloney and liverwurst cold cuts, and German-style potato salad. Pickles, mustard and horseradish garnishments were on the side. Finally, there was Limburger cheese, which I would spread onto two pieces of Rubel's pumpernickel rye and put a thick slice of onion on top. It was one of my favorite sandwiches, even though it's pungent smell often lingered in the kitchen (and on my breath) for hours.

Mom was always there to help me out whenever I needed it, and I was much closer to her emotionally than I was to my father. But she also could get angry with me for some stupid thing I did and wouldn't talk to me for a day or two, but usually I deserved her punishment. One of her favorite pastimes was playing cards, and she was often able to talk my friends and my sister Claire's friends into playing whenever they visited. In those small gatherings she became the life of the party. Over the years she continued to entice visitors to play cards, and even got my children to play when she was babysitting them. Of course, she would win more often than not. In fact, she had such a reputation for playing cards that my sister Claire had three or four playing cards etched into her tombstone. (Dad has a cigar etched on his.)

Despite all the hard work she performed, Mom laughed a lot, and enjoyed activities like going to bingo at Saint Bonnies on Thursday nights, or participating in parish clubs and organizations. Her family and Saint Bonnies were the two pillars around which her life revolved. In 1982 she and my father celebrated their 50th wedding anniversary, and for a gift all the children got together and honored them with a trip to Hawaii—providing them the honeymoon they were too poor to take when they were first married in those early days of the Great Depression.

I had spent the previous summer at the University of Hawaii, so I knew the island of Oahu quite well, and I met them there and guided them around the island. I took them to various sights, and we attended a luau and watched Hawaiian hula dancers, which Mom really enjoyed. One day I drove them around the island, stopping at various sites on the trip, such as the Pali Cliffs, a famous battle site of early Hawaii. As we were getting back into the car, Dad said, "Well, Vee, would you like to move to Hawaii?"

"It's beautiful here," she said, "but I want to go back home, because all my friends live in South Fairmount, and I would miss them too much if I lived here."

So, they returned home to the world they knew and loved. Both of them were now in their early seventies. They seemed to be healthy, and they were looking forward to their retirement years. Little did any of us realize then that inside a year and a half they would both be dead and buried. Dad had a stroke and passed away on September 6, 1983, and Mom followed him, a month to the day, on October 6, 1983. Her official cause of death was congestive heart failure, but the doctor said informally that she had died of a broken heart, and there is undoubtedly some truth to that. The evening she died she had gone bowling with my sister Claire at Saint Bonnies, where she bowled one of the best three-game series of her life. After Claire dropped her off she was walking to the house when her next-door neighbor, Ruth Fluegeman, saw her and invited her in for a cup of tea.

"No thanks," said Mom, "I'm not feeling too good right now, so I'll just go home and rest."

The following morning my sister Claire discovered Mom dead on the bathroom floor.

IN THE GARDEN OF SHADOWS

My parents lie side by side in the morning
shade of this great tree, their headstones marking
their names and date in a time that is no more.
Together they lie in their bed of earth,
companions in death as they were in life,
facing eternity, husband and wife.

In the evening, after the world has spun
a few degrees and the tree no longer
shadows their graves, Mom and Dad now rest
in the soft warm glow of the setting sun
and now they sleep in a peace without strife,
facing eternity, husband and wife.

Garden of Shadows.

6

SAINT BONNIES

*Education is not preparation
for life; education is life itself.*

~ John Dewey

Our local parish church was the central organizing institution in South Fairmount in the 1940s and '50s. In addition to providing a place for worship, the parish church was also the center of educational and social activities. In our case, that church was the Catholic church of Saint Bonaventure or, as we affectionately called it, "Saint Bonnies." It was there that elementary school students like me attended Mass daily during the school year, received our education, went to church festivals, joined social clubs, played in the band, went to bingo on Thursday nights, and bowled in its bowling alleys in the basement of the grade school.

By the time I was born across the street from Saint Bonnies in 1941, the church had been standing for more than seventy years. Around 1840 Bishop Purcell of Cincinnati began recruiting missionaries from Europe to come to Cincinnati to administer to the rising number of German Catholics immigrating there. He convinced German-speaking Franciscan priests from Bozen, a Tyrolean town in Austria (now Bolzano, in northern Italy), to send missionaries to Cincinnati around 1844. In 1869 some of those Franciscans who spoke German came to South Fairmount. Their task was to assume the ministry of the newly constructed church officially known as Saint Bonaventura. A few years later an elementary school was built, and Franciscan nuns began bilingual instruction of children from kindergarten through the eighth grade.

Saint Bonaventure Church, c.1993.

For the next 134 years Saint Bonnies administered the spiritual, educational and social needs of its parishioners. Ultimately, however, repair issues, financial problems and dwindling attendance brought about the church's demise. It closed its doors after the final Mass on June 15, 2003, and the structure was demolished the following year, much to the dismay of many of its former parishioners.

It's not clear why a church dedicated to serving a German American population would be named after an Italian saint and scholar, but perhaps the answer is that Saint Bonaventure was a Franciscan priest. Records also indicate that Bonaventure was a favorite saint of the first Franciscan pastor of the new church, Father Jacob Menchen, also a scholar, who perhaps had enough influence to have the church dedicated to him.

Saint Bonaventure (1221-1274) was an early follower of Saint Francis of Assisi, the founder of the Franciscan Order. Bonaventure eventually rose to become the minister general of the Franciscans, a cardinal, and a Doctor of the Church. Historians of the Middle Ages consider him and Saint Thomas Aquinas to be the two greatest Catholic scholars and theologians of the 13th Century.

Painted on our church's dome above the altar was the image of Saint Bonaventure, accompanied by a quote from the Book of Wisdom:

> "I have loved Wisdom and have sought her out from my youth and desired to take her as my spouse and I have become a lover of her beauty." (*Wisdom*, viii, 2)

I read that quote almost daily from the time I was six until I was fourteen, not knowing then how significant it was to become later in my life, when I too became a scholar—although my meager scholarship was minuscule compared to the quantity and quality of Bonaventure's.

Many of the families in my neighborhood in the 1940s and '50s were of German descent, and Catholic as well. Some of these families were the working-class descendants of the original German settlers who moved west out of the city of Cincinnati, crossed the Mill Creek, and began to settle in this pleasant valley around 1820.

Our neighbors were pretty much alike in class and social standing, and everyone knew one another and participated in similar activities. Many of us rarely ventured out of the neighborhood except to take the streetcar downtown to go shopping in the big department stores, or to walk two miles or so to Crosley Field to watch the Reds play. All in all, ours was pretty much a closed neighborhood, a kind of German-Catholic village, and this culture was the only one I knew for the first seventeen years of my life.

While many of my generation ultimately left South Fairmount and lived our adult lives elsewhere, most of my parents' generation had spent practically their whole lives as members of Saint Bonnies' parish. My mother, Alvina, serves as a good example: she was born on Selim Avenue within a mile of the church, was baptized there, went to school there, made her First Communion there, was married there, celebrated her fiftieth wedding anniversary there, and had her funeral there. Indeed, the Catholic Church was so central to our lives that sometimes I thought we were Catholics first and Americans second. We learned to classify people into two categories, Catholics and Protestants. Even the public school up the block was referred to as "The Protestant school." I rarely heard it called by its real name, Roosevelt School.

Kindergarten

My formal education began when I entered kindergarten at Saint Bonnies in September 1946, just a few days after my fifth birthday. That first day was fraught with anxiety, as I remember crying and resisting the attempts of Sister Mary John to separate me from my mother, onto whose dress I clung for dear life, begging Mom to take me back home with her. That episode probably lasted only a minute or two, but for me it seemed an eternity. Eventually Mom pried my hand from her dress and transferred it to Sister John.

"Stop this now, and go with Sister," Mom says.

Immediately I feel betrayed and abandoned by my mother. As Sister John takes me by the arm and pulls me away, I look back over my shoulder and see that Mom has already turned her back and is walking to the exit door. Sister John practically drags me into the kindergarten classroom.

"Sit down here and stop crying," she demands, "none of the other kids are crying, and if you continue everyone will think you are a baby."

Still upset that my mother had abandoned me, I sit in my seat and pout for a while and finally dry my eyes on my shirt sleeve. Then, after a minute or two, I summon up the courage to go to the small sandbox in the back of the room. As I begin playing there, a little girl comes by and talks to me.

"Don't worry," she says, "maybe kindergarten will be fun."

Her words are a comfort, and that act endears me to her. She tells me her name is Linda Delseno, and I consider her my kindergarten girlfriend from that moment on, although she might not have the same feelings for me. It's my first experience in puppy love. Her words console me enough to know that someone else empathizes with my situation and that I am not alone. The event's strong emotional impact on me is supported by the fact that 75 years later I still remember her name, and that pleasant sandbox moment seems like it happened only yesterday.

Reading and Writing

After the disaster of my first day of kindergarten, school became much more agreeable, so much so that it became a haven for me, a kind of refuge where I began to learn new things and express myself. Separation from my mother and the life I had previously known had been a traumatic experience, yet it was a necessary act that disconnected me from my infancy and early childhood. And my initial resistance to formal education was rather ironic, since I was to spend practically the next seventy years of my life in the classroom, first as a student, and then later as a professor.

In the first grade I became aware of the importance of words and books. Our first *Dick and Jane* readers contained stories designed to increase our knowledge of new words and how they can be joined together into sentences to express ideas by using the first grammatical device taught to us: subject-verb-object. This was my introduction to language and literature, which have been a central part of my life ever since.

It was also during this time in the first and second grades that we were taught the fundamentals of penmanship. We began by using a #2 lead pencil, and we would spend hours learning to write out the alphabet, tracing each letter over and over: AAA aaa, BBB bbb, CCC ccc, and so on, over and over, again and again. That sounds monotonous, but I found that I enjoyed the experience, and I was never bored by it.

By the third grade we had advanced to wooden desktops with a hole in the upper right-hand corner that served as an inkwell, and the nuns provided each of us a bottle of ink and a pen with copper-colored nibs. I loved dipping my pen into the ink and transferring the ink to the paper and creating letters and words, even though sometimes it became a very messy undertaking, especially if the nib dripped ink before you could get it to the page. We all lived in fear of the ink dripping on our desk, or worse, blotting our paper so badly that we had to start over again. Even worse was my fear of getting the ink on my clothes. When that happened there was hell to pay. Mom would throw a fit and wonder if it would come out in the wash, and even if it didn't, I'd still have to wear that shirt again to school and advertise my sloppiness to my teachers and classmates.

Regardless, I grew to love the flow of the ink and the formation of words on the page. There seemed to be something magical about the act of transferring my thoughts onto a piece of paper, and I was very careful in correctly shaping the letters and words. I wanted my words to look nice on the page so others could read them easily. I enjoyed writing and reading more than anything else I did while in grade school, and by the time I was eight I was writing daily in cursive. Unfortunately, cursive is now an almost forgotten style of handwriting, a lost art of penmanship in this new age of computers and cell phones.

In my beginning was the word. In those early years I began to realize, in my budding consciousness, that instead of playing with building blocks, I could play with words, putting them down on paper, building sentences out of them, and rearranging them to make them reveal more possibilities. I don't mean to imply that I apprehended everything that was happening to me as I played with words, for my mind was still developing as I unknowingly struggled out of the darkness of ignorance into the dawn of understanding—and that understanding was more felt than comprehended. Or perhaps it was both felt and comprehended at the same time, and that is how I came to know things, through a union of my intuition and my intellect.

By the time we reached the 5th or 6th grade one of our books was always a reader that was designed to introduce us to new words and ideas in an ever-expanding system. Sometimes on Friday afternoons our teacher would have us line up on either side of the classroom. Each student would have to read aloud a passage or paragraph from the book. If you made a pronunciation mistake or stumbled over a new word, you would be disqualified and have to sit down.

Then someone on the other side of the classroom had to do the same, and it became a competition between the two sides, or teams, and the last boy or girl standing would win for their team. I loved competing in this educational game and was always eager to get up and read. I made very few mistakes and was, now and then, the last person standing. I also discovered that I enjoyed reading aloud, giving voice to the words on the page. Although I had no idea of it at the time, I'm sure this is where I developed my love of language, literature and performance, and these classroom contests prepared me for the scholarly and dramatic work that would occupy much of my adult life.

Early on I became aware that I was a pretty good writer, and now and then the nuns would compliment me on my work. At first I didn't think much of such praise because I didn't think myself worthy of it. I thought that if I could write this way, then it was obvious that everyone else could do the same. But as I grew older I came to realize that wasn't the case.

In the sixth or seventh grade we saw a film in the auditorium that was sponsored by the Cincinnati Gas and Electric Company, and each student was required to write and submit a little review of the film. It would be judged by the nuns, and the best essays were submitted to the company to be judged along with all the essays that other schools city-wide had submitted.

Anita Broering was always the smartest person in our class, and the nuns chose her paper for the girls' submission, and mine for the boys'. Unfortunately, neither of our essays received any recognition on the city level, and the incident was soon forgotten. Still, I find it curious that, considering where I ended up in life, my first important writing experience was a review of a film! A dozen years later I would be in college writing film reviews for the *Xavier News*. And a few years after that I would be a university professor teaching film history, and writing and publishing critical essays on motion pictures.

As I grew older I came to believe that life presents to each of us signs, or certain options and possibilities, that reveal where our life is meant to go, even if we don't realize it at the time. I believe that this grade-school essay was one of those signs that unconsciously prompted me to continue writing.

There were other things to learn at school. Arithmetic was not my favorite subject, although I did well enough in it, but I just didn't find it as interesting as reading and writing. History was interesting, and I especially enjoyed stories of the Civil War and the two World Wars. One year during Lent a nun—I think it was Sister Mary Quentin—taught us about the various churches located in Rome's Vatican City. She provided us with maps of the Holy City that she had mimeographed and handed out to the class. We would plot out each church and its importance during the six weeks of Lent, ending with the crowning architectural glory, Saint Peter's Basilica.

Built over 400 years earlier, Saint Peter's was the most important church of Catholicism, and the home church of Pope Pius XII, whose portrait hung in every classroom of our school. Sister Quentin showed us photos of Saint Peter's, and she told us that even though this was the greatest church in the world, anyone was allowed to go to Mass there, even us, if we were ever to visit Rome. But that would be nearly impossible, she said, since Rome was thousands of miles away, and none of our parents had the money to take us there. Yet, less than ten years later, in December 1961, I was twenty years old and in the Navy on a ship homeported in Naples, Italy, and two of my shipmates and I took a train to Rome and attended Christmas Mass at Saint Peter's. Funny how these things work out, isn't it?

One of the best parts of school for me were the stories we read about other people and places from around the world that stirred our imagination and opened up new worlds for us, worlds beyond the valley in which we lived. One day in 1953, for example, Mr. Hornickel visited our sixth-grade classroom. He had owned a grocery store down on Queen City Avenue, but suddenly, as if he had seen the future, he closed his grocery store and opened an appliance store and began selling TVs.

To our surprise, Mr. Hornickel brought a TV into our class and plugged it in, and within minutes we were watching the coronation of Queen Elizabeth II on TV. I wondered why Mr. Hornickel would go out of his way to do this, but I later decided that his goal was to advertise his new TV business, and that we would go home and tell our parents about it, and they would go down and buy a TV from him.

My Ticket to Paradise

The warm Friday afternoon sun filters through the stained-glass windows into the nave of Saint Bonnies church, sprinkling the pews and aisles with the soft colors of the rainbow, while the aromas of candle wax and incense from the morning Mass linger in the air. It's May 1949, and I'm seven years old, standing in line with my classmates from the second grade, all of us waiting to undergo our first confession, which we are required to do before making our First Communion the following Sunday.

The nuns have organized us into two lines on each side of the church as we await our turn in the confessional booth. For the next few minutes I stand silently in line, filled with anxiety as I try to recall the sins I've committed, even though I'm just seven years old. I can only remember about two or three "bad things" I've done, such as lying, or not obeying my parents, or stealing a nickel from my mom's purse so I could buy a popsicle, or maybe a pack of candy cigarettes.

I'm afraid the priest will find my confession inadequate, since I have very few sins to report. So, while I stand in line awaiting my turn in the booth, I decide to make up a few extra sins so the priest would be satisfied and give me absolution, thereby wiping away all the sins from my soul so that I would be pure and holy when I received my First Communion. I didn't realize it then, but by reporting sins I didn't even commit was, in fact, lying to the priest—which was another sin!

We've been instructed to walk inside this dark little booth and kneel down and tell this man concealed behind a screen all the sins we have committed. He is, after all, a priest of the Roman Catholic Church, God's representative here on Earth, and therefore it's my duty to reveal to him all my sins, both venial sins (small moral infractions, like lying) and mortal sins, those terrible sins like murder that, if not confessed to a priest before one died, would result in that person being damned to Hell for all eternity.

I enter the confessional and kneel down facing a small window with a dense screen and a small door. Immediately the small door slides open on the other side of the screen. I can't see through the screen, but I can make out the profile of the priest's head, which immediately whispers, "In the name of the Father, and of the Son, and of the Holy Ghost, Amen." Instantly I recognize the voice as that of Father Jerome, one of my favorite priests because, unlike most other priests, he is always good natured and informal when he visits us in class. My anxiety lessens, and I begin my first confession as I had been instructed: "Bless me, Father, for I have sinned...."

I then tell Father Jerome my few sins, both the real ones and the ones I made up, after which he tells me I am forgiven, and encourages me to try to be good in the future. Then he tells me to pray three "Hail Marys" as my penance. As I leave the confessional I feel happy and relieved now that my soul is cleansed of all sin, and I think of the three milk bottle diagrams in the *Baltimore Catechism* that stand for a soul. One bottle of white milk indicates that the soul is free of all sins; one bottle with black dots in it illustrates venial sins; and the one totally black bottle indicates that this soul has committed a mortal sin. For now, at least, I thought my soul was a clear bottle of white milk.

The nuns and priests had prepared us well for confession, teaching us how to examine our conscience and be our own policeman, confessing what crimes we had committed, assessing our own guilt, and feeling shame for ourselves and our imperfections. Yet, that was a small price to pay, as the priests and nuns reminded us, because confession was our ticket to Paradise. If I went to confession and was absolved of my sins, and soon after if I was crossing the street and an automobile struck and killed me, I would go directly to Heaven, where I would be happy for all eternity with God, Jesus, Mary and all the saints that had gone before. But, while Heaven might be something to wish for, I certainly didn't want to go there any time soon as a result of being accidentally run over by a car!

Sister Mary Theresa, our second-grade teacher, had spent much of the year since September preparing us for our first confession and our First Communion that coming May, that special event that would make us full participants in the Catholic Church and the "Mystical Body of Christ," even though I really didn't understand what that meant. There was a lot about religion that I didn't understand at that age, but I was told not to worry about it. All I had to do was believe it.

Sister Theresa began by introducing us to the *Baltimore Catechism*, the official handbook outlining the basics of Catholic theology. The book's format consisted of questions and answers that we were supposed to memorize and make part of our lives. The first question was perhaps the most important:

<u>Question</u>: *What is the purpose of life?*

<u>Answer</u>: *To know, love and serve God, and be happy with Him in Heaven.*

That was all. It didn't matter who you were, what job you had, or where you lived. All that mattered is that you followed the teaching of the Church as outlined in the *Baltimore Catechism*.

I didn't know much about God, really, except that he lived in Heaven, which was somewhere up there beyond the clouds. At that young age my faith was newborn and feeble, so I tried to do what I was told, and I tried to love God as best I could, even though I really didn't know how to love someone I couldn't see, especially someone who never seemed to have time to answer my prayers. Early on I sometimes wondered that if God didn't have time to come down and talk to me personally, couldn't He at least maybe just send me a letter in the mail? But I was only seven, so what did I know? At least I did know what it meant to serve Him, which is what I tried to do by living my life the way the nuns and priests trained me, and I continued to do so, more or less, for the next twenty years.

School Days

"Time to get up!"

Mom calls from downstairs, rousing me from my slumber on this cold winter morning. I linger in my warm bed for a few minutes longer, knowing that my older brothers and sister would commandeer the bathroom anyway. But five minutes later Dad calls, this time more insistently, "Don't make me come up there!" he threatens. I know better than to defy him, because if he does come up, he'll feel obligated to pull me out of bed and spank me, which he has done more than once. So, I reluctantly crawl out of my warm bed. Shivering in the cold attic, I quickly throw on some school clothes and go downstairs to wash my face and hands in the bathroom before I enter the warm kitchen for breakfast.

Today Mom has made for us a breakfast of scrambled eggs with a side of goetta, which she had made a couple of days before by boiling down the ingredients (pork shoulder, pinhead oatmeal and spices) for a few hours, and when they congealed she shaped them into loaves, put them into bread pans, and refrigerated them overnight. In the morning she would fry enough slices for all of us. When the goetta was fried just right, with the edges seared crisp, the slices were delicious and worth getting out of bed for.

I finish breakfast by 7:30 and throw on my coat, hat and gloves and get ready to head off to eight o'clock Mass at Saint Bonnies. It had snowed overnight, so I wedge my shoes into dilapidated, over-sized galoshes that were hand-me-downs from my older brothers. The goulashes have holes in them, but I wrap over the holes with Scotch tape, hoping that the temporary fix will last until I got to church, and my shoes and socks wouldn't get soaked.

It's January 1951, and I'm only nine years old. The snow's ankle-deep, and my cheeks are blistered by the wind as I begin to walk a mile to school in freezing temperatures. I start my trek on Westwood Avenue by the Spring Garden Bank. I walk west toward Shadwell Park, entering the park at the eastern gate on Westwood Avenue, directly across the street from Hoffmann's Café at the bottom of Selim Avenue.

Then I trudge across the wind-swept frozen tundra of the park, imagining I'm in Alaska and a polar bear is hiding behind the swimming pool. I'm always trying to avoid those thin sheets of ice that would give way under my weight and expose my boots to the puddles of water underneath. I exit the park though the tennis court gate at the intersection of Grand and Queen City Avenues and walk past Rebold's Funeral Home.

After ten minutes I'm already chilled to the bone. Tears well up in my eyes from the cold, my nose drips mucus, my fingertips freeze to the first knuckles, and my earlobes sting like they have needles stuck in them.

Wondering how Eskimos can tolerate such a life, I continue up Queen City Avenue for two more blocks of freezing misery, past the house where the Luken twins live, past Ken and Jimmy Mahon's house and Elmer Hoffmann's paint store, then past the high wall of Saint Bonnies' school yard and into church at last, where warmth and lighted candles and the bittersweet aroma of incense greet me. Even though the church is a sanctuary of warmth during the frigid days of winter, it still takes a couple of minutes before my numb fingers are warm and flexible enough to open my daily missal and follow the prayers that were part of the Mass.

During the Mass the nuns periodically stroll up and down the aisles, like policemen on patrol, making sure our noses are in our missals. At times a boy who is goofing around or nodding off to sleep receive a sharp smack on the back of the neck with an angry reprimand, "PAY ATTENTION – OR ELSE!" The rest of us lower our heads into our missals in fear of a similar punishment. At the same time, we slyly eye our classmates kneeling nearby, silently sharing our delight because the class bully is himself being bullied by the nuns.

On the first Friday of every month it's virtually mandatory that we fast from food after midnight so we can participate in Holy Communion. When we rise in the morning we're not allowed to eat breakfast. At most, we're permitted only a sip of water to quench our thirst before leaving home. Before I enter church I stop across the street at Moellinger's Bakery to buy two chocolate-covered donuts that cost maybe five cents each. Then I carry the donuts in a paper bag into the church, and I place the bag atop my books in my pew seat. All during the Mass my stomach growls from hunger, while the savory smell of the donuts rising from the bag makes my mouth water in anticipation.

Finally, and not a moment too soon, the choir sings the *Agnus Dei* and Communion time begins. We walk in line up to the Communion rail where the priest serves us the host, the body of Christ, and then we return to our pews. After Communion is over the Mass soon ends, and the students walk together, two-by-two, to the school's lunchroom, where I buy a pint jar of orange drink. I take ten minutes to eat my donuts and drink my juice, and then around 9 a.m., my stomach satisfied at least for now, I return to my homeroom, and classes begin.

Ceremonies and Rituals

Lent begins every year around the middle of February, starting on Ash Wednesday, when the priest smudges ashes on our foreheads with the sign of the cross, reminding us that we came from ashes and will return to ashes when we die. The period lasts forty days until Good Friday, and it is the most somber period of the church calendar, culminating in the joyous celebration of Easter.

Lent's not a time for fun. It's a gloomy period of self-imposed denial, called fasting, and we're encouraged by the nuns to pledge that we will abstain from such pleasures as candy and comic books and movies. Most of us start out with good intentions to deny ourselves these treats for forty days, but within a week or two we break our pledges and succumb to the profane lures of candy and comics and movies. Those students who claim they have kept their pledges for all forty days of Lent are usually girls seeking favor from the nuns, but the rest of us know that those girls are probably lying anyway.

Throughout Lent our schedule is Mass every weekday morning, as usual. In addition, on Friday afternoons school ends a half-hour early so all the classes, first grade to eighth, can file back into church to witness and participate in the Way of the Cross, the fourteen-station ceremony depicting the final days of Christ, from his condemnation by Pontius Pilate to his crucifixion and entombment.

Each station is marked by a bas-relief sculpture mounted on the walls of the church depicting a scene leading to Christ's death, narrating the story of The Way of the Cross. The priest stops to pray at every station, beginning with, "We adore Thee, oh Christ, and we praise Thee," to which the congregation responds, "For by Thy cross Thou hast redeemed the world."

This portrayal of Christ's last days became one of my favorite rituals. I didn't realize it then, but I think I was attracted to it because it was so dramatic. And even by the time I was eight years old I was disappointed that it took place within the confines of the church, and not outside in the streets. If it were performed outside, I thought, we could have actors play Christ and Mary and the other figures in this drama, with the climax being the crucifixion of Christ.

* * * * *

I finally fulfilled this early idea forty years later in the mid-1990s, when my partner Carol Ann and I staged The Way of the Cross on Good Friday every year for four years in the streets of Camden, New Jersey, known then as the drug and murder capital of America. A thriving city in the 1940s, Camden had begun to deteriorate after World War II. As a result of that decline came poverty, race riots, drugs and gang-related assassinations. This was, I thought, the perfect place to dramatize the last days of Christ.

By 1994 the Catholic Church of Our Lady of Fatima in Camden was comprised primarily of parishioners who had recently emigrated from Puerto Rico, Mexico, and Central America. They had replaced earlier generations of Italian parishioners who had moved up to the middle class and vacated Camden for the suburbs of southern New Jersey.

When I approached the pastor of the church, Father Salvatore, with the idea of staging the Way of the Cross, he was enthusiastic, and provided me with all the support I needed. But he told me that many of the parishioners who would participate barely spoke English, so that might be a problem. As I constructed the dialogue between Christ and Pilate, I recalled that when Christ was crucified the ruling authorities were Roman and spoke Latin, while the Jews spoke Aramaic. I decided to duplicate that language relationship in our production: Pilate would speak English, the dominant language of our society, while Christ and the High Priests spoke Spanish, a secondary language. Since most of the people in the audience spoke Spanish as their primary language, they would be able to follow the spoken exchange between Pilate and Christ much easier.

One day during rehearsals I approached one of the actors, Rafael, who was playing a minor role as a Roman soldier. I gave him a harmless theatrical hand whip to strike Christ with when he fell. The first time we rehearsed the fall, Rafael approached the actor who was playing Christ and very gently brushed the whip across his back. I stopped the rehearsal and said, "Rafael, you have to really whip him hard."

"No," he said, "that is Jesus."

"No, he's not Jesus," I said. "That's your friend, Roberto. He's *playing* Jesus. And, if it were really Jesus, He would want you to whip him hard anyway. Besides, with this whip you won't really hurt him. You just have to act like you are hurting him."

It was as if a veil had been lifted from Rafael's consciousness. His eyes grew large, and he turned to look at me with a smile of understanding. When we rehearsed the scene once again, Rafael flayed Christ hard across his back two or three times, and he, Roberto and I were all satisfied.

After three weeks of rehearsals, Good Friday finally arrived. I gathered all the actors together in the church's dressing room and wished them well and encouraged them to have a good performance. As they exited the dressing room, I pulled Rafael aside and I reminded him to whip Christ hard. He smiled at me and nodded.

For the next hour Father Sal led the procession through the streets of Camden, saying the prayers at each station. At the same time, I went to an empty lot where there was a large dirt mound about six feet high, upon which we would crucify Christ. Since I was preparing the mound for the crucifixion to happen, I wasn't able to watch the procession as it passed through the neighborhood streets. When the procession came to the dirt mound we crucified the actor playing Christ (no, we did not put nails through his hands or wrists, but our staging was still very realistic). About two hundred people stood by and witnessed the crucifixion.

After the dramatization of the Way of the Cross was over the crowd dispersed and the actors returned to the dressing room. I then approached Rafael and asked him if he had whipped Christ hard.

"Yes," he said. "But when I did, one of the biggest drug dealers in Camden stepped out of the crowd and walked up to me and said, 'If you do that once more to Jesus, I'll come out here and bust both your knees!'"

"Did you tell him that that wasn't really Jesus?" I asked.

"No," Rafael said. "I didn't say anything. I just didn't whip Jesus anymore."

And that's the true story of how one of the biggest drug dealers in Camden, New Jersey, came to the defense of Christ and tried to protect him from harm while on his way to his crucifixion!

*Way of the Cross re-enactment, Camden, New Jersey, 1994.
Photo by Carol Ann DeSimine.*

* * * * *

Now that I look back with a clearer head and heart, I recognize how much I enjoyed those rituals and ceremonies that brought our congregation together, even though, like most kids, I was impatient and lazy, and I sometimes thought of them primarily as events I was made to suffer through. There were memorable ceremonies, like Midnight Mass on Christmas Eve, where hundreds of parishioners crammed shoulder to shoulder into St. Bonnies, their collective body heat warming the church.

When it snows or rains on Christmas Eve, the coats of the parishioners emit a light condensation as they dry in the warmth of the church, and that misty vapor, mixed with the smoke of the incense, hangs a few feet above us like a translucent cloud. The atmosphere is solemn, yet joyous.

Colorful poinsettia plants and Christmas trees decorate the altar as we experience the pageantry of the priests and the spectacle of the Latin Solemn High Mass, while the choir sings traditional hymns like "Silent Night," "*Adestes Fedelis*," and many others, all under the direction of our renowned choir director, Omer Westendorf.

Once Midnight Mass is over we linger on the front steps of the church and exchange Christmas greetings with our friends and neighbors. Then we walk home in the cold at 1:30 a.m. in the morning, and open our Christmas presents while Mom prepares a late-night breakfast of scrambled eggs and bacon. She encourages us to drink a glass of Manischewitz wine with our meal—"My Cincinnati Jewish wine," she calls it. Ironically, Christmas is the only day of the year we have wine with our meals, and it's a Jewish wine! But to me the wine tastes bitter and makes me shiver when I sip it, so I fill my wine glass with Coca-Cola instead.

The meal ends by 2:30 a.m. and drowsiness sets in. My brothers and sisters and I go upstairs to our bedrooms in the attic to snuggle against the cold beneath our featherbed covers. Meanwhile, Dad descends into the chilly basement and shovels enough coal into the furnace to warm the house through the night, and we dream the hours away knowing all is safe and happy in our little world.

Then, too, there was Easter, and the Holy Days of Obligation, and the feast days of saints that needed to be celebrated. One of my favorite feasts took place in early May every year where we honored Mary, the mother of Christ. Led by Omer Westendorf on the organ, we sang wonderful songs with such lyrics as "Oh, Mary, we crown thee with blossoms today / Queen of the angels, Queen of the May…." I can still recall the aroma of flowers mixed with incense and burning candle wax as a four-foot statue of Mary was carried around the church on a pallet and then out into the streets, where we participated in a procession that wound through the neighborhood.

In May of 1955, a month before my graduation from Saint Bonnies, I was selected by the nuns to be one of the four bearers of the pallet that transported the statue of Mary during the May parade. I was happy and proud to be given such a prestigious position and responsibility. My mother was in the crowd of bystanders by the Vitt and Stermer Funeral Home and took a photo of me as I passed by shouldering the statue's pallet, a photo I cherish in this album of memories.

Parade honoring Blessed Virgin Mary, 1955. I'm in the back, closest to the camera.

Classroom Crimes

It's April 1954, and I'm sitting at my desk in my seventh-grade classroom at Saint Bonnies with the other students, facing our teacher, a Franciscan nun whose name I no longer remember. So here I will call her Sister Mary Lawrence, and while that wasn't her real name, the events I describe here really happened.

Behind her, just above the blackboard, are the portraits of Pope Pius XII and President Dwight D. Eisenhower. The pope sits in his chair with his right hand outstretched and with two fingers up, as if he were ordering a cup of coffee at a restaurant. But it's really supposed to be a blessing he is giving us. His stern eyes look directly at me, and his lips are pursed as if he is accusing me of some sin. Each time I look at him I feel guilt and shame. I wonder, since he's God's representative here on Earth, if he too is omnipotent and can see me now, this lowly sinner, sitting here in the classroom. I want him to like me, but there's nothing in his face that makes me feel as if he cares for me at all.

The portrait of President Eisenhower makes me feel much better because he has a faint smile on his face, as if he is assuring me that everything will be alright and there's nothing to worry about. I believe him. After all, he almost single-handedly won the war against the Nazis and saved democracy—at least that's what the nuns taught us. While the pope was the Holy Father, President Eisenhower was more of a regular father figure, or at least an "Uncle Ike."

Still, no matter how much his image comforted us, we all knew that the Cold War with the godless Russian Communists was still going on, and every now and then we'd practice the Atomic Bomb air raid drill, hiding beneath our desks, hoping and praying that if the bomb exploded it would somehow miss us, and that Sister Lawrence would then dismiss the class so we could go out and play.

Above these two portraits of the Pope and the President is the image of Christ hanging from the crucifix, a constant reminder of the corporal pain and suffering He underwent to ensure our salvation and save us from an eternity of suffering in Hell. But rather than feeling thankful, I can only feel guilt whenever I look at the cross, since the nuns told me that it was my sins that put Jesus there.

To me, Sister Lawrence is two different women. A heavy-set woman in her late thirties who suffers from failing eyesight, she often looks like gloom and doom when she walks the school's hallways, but when she sits behind her desk and speaks to us about her love for Jesus she removes her thick glasses and slowly turns toward the window and the sky outside, and her face assumes an angelic aura, as if she were already in Heaven. Apparently she can see things out that window that we can't. Maybe it's because she isn't wearing her glasses.

One day she told us that the vows she took when she became a nun were like marriage vows, and that she considered herself the bride of Christ, for no other man could give her the perfect love He provided. Christ was her paragon of love, her spiritual husband. And she often reminded us that our ability to love was woefully inferior to His. Disheartened, I felt guilty and inadequate for not being able to live up to her high standards.

Moments later, when Sister Lawrence returns from her heavenly reveries, she puts her glasses back on and faces us with a warm smile, and we know she will be nice to us for the rest of the day. Yet we're all aware that she might arrive in class tomorrow and be her other self, as mean and intimidating as a bulldog, keeping us prisoners while teaching us catechism in her flowing black habit and cowl with a white starched bib, or wimple, that extended a foot below her chin. Her outfit covers every inch of her body except her hands and face.

Sister Lawrence is the local extension of the Pope's authority, and the classroom is her domain. An experienced teacher, she wields her power judiciously, although she is always quick to employ it whenever necessary. She has a variety of punishments that she administers when the occasion demands. For small transgressions, like not paying attention or being late for morning Mass, the punishment might be slight, like staying after school to sponge clean the blackboards and slap the erasers together out the window to get rid of all the chalk dust. Such a detention isn't too bad, although it does delay us from getting out of school and playing with our friends.

The goal of her second level of punishment is to shame miscreant students in front of the class, to make an example of their misbehavior as a warning to the rest of us not to do the same. One day a girl made the mistake of wearing lipstick to class, and Sister Lawrence grew furious when she saw her. Ushering her to the front of the classroom, she humiliates the girl by giving her a tissue and ordering her to wipe off her lipstick in front of us. Then she grabs the girl's purse and pulls out her lipstick tube. Holding the tube up in front of the class, Sister Lawrence slowly turns the dial on the tube until the lipstick appears.

"Do any of you know what this lipstick is made of?" she asks.

No one volunteers an answer. Given the circumstances, and in the face of her anger, we're all too afraid to respond.

"The answer is that lipstick is made out of crushed lice!" she exclaims. "So, boys, remember this: if you ever have the desire to kiss a girl who is wearing lipstick, don't do it! She's wearing *crushed lice!*"

Several of the boys, including me, instinctively lift our shirt cuffs to our mouths and wipe our lips in disgust, swearing to ourselves, if only for a moment, never to kiss a girl who wore lipstick—although at twelve years of age we certainly are itching to try. After all, in the movies Humphrey Bogart kissed Ingrid Bergman when she wore lipstick, and he didn't seem to mind. I wanted to kiss Ingrid Bergman, too. And my mother wore lipstick when she went out to play bingo on Thursday nights–did that mean Dad wasn't supposed to kiss Mom that night? I'm confused. But that was Sister Lawrence's goal: to confuse us, especially when it had to do with our budding sexual identities.

Finally, for the worst crimes she administers corporal punishment. Like all Franciscan nuns, she wears a white rope tied around her black habit at the waist that serves as a belt. About a half-inch in diameter, it's similar to the cotton rope Mom uses for her clothesline in our backyard. The end of the rope hangs down her right side to just below her knees, and equally spaced along the rope are three knots, each symbolizing the vows the Franciscan nuns and priests took upon their investiture: Poverty, Chastity and Obedience. Those vows are the rules she practices, both in her private life and in the classroom. And she wants us to practice them as well.

I already know about poverty, since it's pretty much part of my everyday life, but I don't enjoy practicing it very much. And chastity? Well, I also try to practice that, too, but my budding sexual impulses at 12 years of age suggest I'm not going to be very successful at chastity. Yet, obedience was the vow Sister Lawrence is concerned with now. For the offending student who disrupts the class by laughing at her, or talking back, or otherwise undermines her authority and classroom discipline, she resorts to corporal punishment. And I'm not simply talking about rapping a student's hands with a ruler. This is far worse.

On those rare occasions when her power is seriously challenged she brings the young miscreant to the front of the class, making the boy (it was always a boy) turn towards his classmates and bend over and put his hands on a desk in the front row. Then she applies the punishment. Grasping the rope around her waist, she whips the boy at least three or four times in front of the entire class, making sure the knots strike his buttocks or upper thighs with enough force to elicit cries of pain and tears.

If the kid is a bully, my first response to his public flogging is to smile at him as he faces us. But that's rare, and most of the time I feel sorry for the victim. After all, he could be me. Still, I always feel that the punishment far outweighs the crime, and I wonder if the crucified Christ hanging on the cross above the blackboard favors the child criminal or his adult abuser. And what does Francis, the saint of peace and kindness, think of such punishment?

After the whippings Sister Lawrence grabs the tearful boy by the scruff of his neck and makes him apologize for disrupting the class. This is her way of implicating us in the boy's punishment. It was our classroom he had disrupted; therefore, we must participate in his punishment by approving it and accepting his apology.

In those day the nuns could administer such physical punishment without reprimand. Since ours was a private Catholic school, the nuns were free to do as they pleased. And we, the victims, had no recourse, for even if we ran home and told our parents that the nun whipped us, our parents might administer additional punishment because we made the nun so angry that she would do things she didn't want to do—like whip us!

Perhaps she had her own past history of physical violence that she had to deal with. I don't know. But by the look on her face when she administered her holy punishment, Sister Lawrence seemed to enjoy whipping those young boys who, as she so often reminded us, would never grow up to be someone's perfect lover, like Christ was for her.

SAINT FRANCIS AND UNCLE AL

In the fourth grade during Holy Week
Sister Mary Joseph led the class
in meditation about Saint Francis.
"Children," she would say, "try to be like him.
Desire to be like him." And we did try.
And on Holy Thursday she stood in front
of the class and had us all pray with her,
pleading with God to grant us, like Francis,
the Stigmata tomorrow, Good Friday.

But most of us prayed with our fingers crossed,
since we were too afraid to be saintly,
just as we are today. And, after all,
we didn't want to bleed from our hands and feet
on Good Fridays for the rest of our lives.

As we prayed I would think of my Uncle Al,
a sad, pickled barfly who never had a dime,
who always told me that without money
a man is nothing in this world, and he
was living proof of his own truth. But I
would tell him that Saint Francis gave all
his money away and lived free with the birds
and animals. "You listened to those nuns
too much and too long," he said, "Saint Francis
was a fool; that's what I learned."

Uncle Al was so busy drowning in drink that he
had little time to think of others. Yet,
one Christmas he somehow got the money
to buy me a red sled with slick runners
and sturdy body, and that night I prayed

beneath my covers to Holy Mary
to bring us snow tomorrow, deep, soft snow
that would cushion me in an accident.

While I slept that night, Mary answered
my prayers, and the next day I thanked her
as we towed our sleds to the very top
of Northside Avenue and hurled ourselves
down the greatest sled slope ever invented,
at least in our neighborhood. And I thanked
Mary once again when I lost control
on my third run and slammed into a huge
snowbank and was entombed for a frozen,
pristine moment, on the edge of what I thought
to be oblivion. My mother laughed
when she saw it happen, a big, rolling
Germanic laugh, rose-cheeked and full of life,
as she ran and dug me out of the snow
and hugged me in the pleasure of knowing
I was not harmed, warming me in her arms,
promising me her cookies and a cup
of hot cocoa when we got home. And then
she taught me how to create snow angels
as we lay on our backs, waving our arms
up and down, and I was so happy then
as the sun smiled down upon us in the
snow-covered foothills of Cincinnati.

But now Mom's gone, and I often think she's
in Heaven, waiting for me to come home,
setting out her warm cookies on my plate
as the cocoa simmers in the pot on the stove.

7

SOUTH FAIRMOUNT

*All memories are sad, because
the past will never come back.*

Shadows in Paradise
~ Erich Maria Remarque

An 1869 map of Cincinnati reveals that Queen City Avenue was then called Lick Run Pike, a road that ran along a stream also named Lick Run. The stream began high up in the western hills and flowed down through a valley that contained various settlements with names like Forbusville, Barrsville, Petersburg and Spring Garden. In later years these areas were combined and came to be known as the neighborhood of South Fairmount.

The valley was nestled between Mount Fairmount to the north, now called St. Clair Heights, Mount Harrison to the southwest, which is now known as Price Hill, and Bald Knob to the southeast. The stream flowed east between Lick Run Pike and Main Street, which is now Westwood Avenue, and continued through this area down to where it joined the Mill Creek, which then flowed south for about a mile and emptied into the Ohio River.

Why Queen City Avenue was then called Lick Run Pike we might never know. The origin of the name seems to have been lost in the past. Some suggest it was called Lick Run because in the wilderness days, long before the white settlers came, there were natural salt deposits along the stream. Deer and buffalo would come to lick the salt deposits and absorb the nutrients they contained. Native tribes like the Shawnee and the Miami, who lived and hunted in the area, undoubtedly found the hunting good all along the stream. Game was plentiful, and a day's hunt usually guaranteed a campfire feast in the evening.

When the first white hunters explored this valley in the early 1800s, they probably learned about the salt licks from the departing Native Americans, and apparently the hunters were the ones who named the stream Lick Run. Considering the importance of the stream, the valley itself became known for a while as Lick Run.

Harrison Turnpike was constructed around 1805. It was named after William Henry Harrison, the famous soldier who had recently participated in the wars against the Native Americans in the Northwest Territories. He was appointed Governor of the Indiana Territory by President Thomas Jefferson in 1801, and he would later be elected President of the United States. Harrison Turnpike ran from Cincinnati across a small bridge over the Mill Creek, and then up the hill on the southern side of Mt. Fairmount and, eventually, all the way to Indiana. Today it's called Harrison Avenue.

By the 1820s immigrants had already begun using the Harrison Turnpike to cross the Mill Creek and settle in the Lick Run valley. Shortly thereafter, German immigrant farmers began to till the soil, while others began planting grape orchards on the valley's hillsides. For the next thirty years or so the grape harvests were bountiful, and the area became part of Cincinnati's famed Catawba Wine country. In addition, dairy farming in the valley was a major enterprise for much of the 19th Century, and between 1870 and 1900 South Fairmount dairies supplied much of the milk for the city of Cincinnati.

The area of Lick Run was annexed by Cincinnati on February 28,1870, a year after Saint Bonaventure Church was constructed. An article in the *Cincinnati Enquirer* indicates that the name of Lick Run Pike was changed to Queen City Avenue by a city ordinance on July 23, 1879, even though later maps, such as the Rand, McNally 1909 map of Cincinnati, continued to refer to Queen City Avenue as Lick Run Pike. In any event, about 140 years ago Queen City Avenue became the main thoroughfare of South Fairmount and remains so to the present day.

South Fairmount was my home for the first 17 years of my life. As a result, I developed a close emotional attachment to the neighborhood, and I came to know it very well. One of the ways I did that was by delivering newspapers.

Paper Boy

I was nine years old in the summer of 1951 when I got my first job, selling newspapers on the corner of Harrison and Beekman Avenues, in front of the #21 Firehouse at the western end of the Western Hills Viaduct. I would sell papers every afternoon to motorists who would stop at the traffic light. Summers were tolerable, but winters froze me to the bone, and many days I would duck inside the firehouse for a few minutes of warmth that would bring blood back into my hands and fingertips, so I could make change for those who bought the newspaper.

Now and then the firemen would let me watch a few minutes of TV on the new television set they had purchased. I got to watch the last few innings of the 1951 All Star Game, which the National League won, 8-3. I watched Stan Musial hit a home run, and my earliest Cincinnati Reds hero, Ewell ("The Whip") Blackwell, pitched the last inning in relief. My most memorable day selling papers came a year later in August 1952, when I stood on the corner holding up the front page, tears rolling down my cheeks as I angrily yelled out to those passing by, "Ewell Blackwell traded to the Yankees!" Being traded was bad enough. But to the dreaded Yankees? That was unforgivable.

Shortly after that I got a new job. Instead of standing on the corner for three hours selling newspapers and making at most 25 cents a day, I switched to delivering newspapers six days a week, Monday through Saturday, though the heart of South Fairmount in 1953 and '54. I picked up my first load of two of the daily papers, the *Cincinnati Post* and the *Cincinnati Times Star* at the firehouse. My bag of about fifty papers was packed by my boss, Angelo Farelli, who had a team of about five delivery boys working for him. They would cover the entire neighborhood. He would start us off at the firehouse and then hop into his dark green Plymouth station wagon and drop off more bundles of papers at designated areas of our routes.

I sling my fully-loaded canvas newspaper bag onto my left shoulder and begin my route down Harrison Avenue, delivering papers to homes along the street, down past Dr. Smith's office at 1506 Harrison (he was the neighborhood doctor who attended my birth a decade before), past Ernie Hammann's Café, Queen Anne's Confectionary, Hader's Hardware store (which once housed South Fairmount's first nickelodeon movie theatre), past Dr. Hirsch's office, behind which Charlie Milazzo lives, down past Lausche's Bakery that sells the tastiest cream-filled "horns" ever, past Ruth Fluegeman's Dry Goods Store, Smith's Shoe Store and, finally, Westermann's Drug Store.

At the traffic light at Harrison and Queen City I turn up Queen City Avenue and continue delivering to homes and stores along the northern, right-hand side of the street, passing the West Hills Theater and Kroger's Supermarket on my left, and then continue past the Water Works and

Shadwell Park until I get to Rebold's Funeral Home on the corner of Queen City and Grand Avenues.

There I load up my bag again with another batch of papers recently dropped off by Angelo and continue up Queen City past Fairmount Hardware and Hoffman's Paint store, past Saint Bonnie's schoolyard and church, past the apartment house at 1805 Queen City Avenue where I was born (though I never knew it then—my parents didn't tell me until I was a teenager!), all the way up to Quebec Road, where it intersects Queen City Avenue at Saint Francis Hospital. It was there that I was to pick up the next batch of papers Angelo had dropped off for me.

Sometimes Angelo is late in supplying this last set of papers (he always blames the traffic). While waiting for him I sit down on the curb and read one of the extra papers left over in my sack. I usually ignore the front pages (those are for older people) and turn directly to the sports section to look up the Reds' box score from last night's game, hoping my hero, Ted Kluszewski ("Big Klu"), had hit a home run or two.

But one day my attention is immediately drawn to the large headlines on the front page. It's August 14, 1953, just three weeks before my 12th birthday, and the headlines shout out that yesterday the Russians exploded a Hydrogen Bomb, reportedly a thousand times more powerful than the Atomic Bomb. The United States had earlier developed the first H-Bomb, but now the Russians had caught up with our weaponry, and the Cold War between the East and West had reached a deep, dark moment: for the first time in the history of mankind two enemy nations each possessed "doomsday weapons" that had the potential of destroying all life on this planet.

It was on those days I sat reading the paper when I first began to understand what was happening outside my little world of South Fairmount.

Over the months I also read about Julius and Ethel Rosenberg being electrocuted for giving atomic bomb secrets to the Russians, and I worried about their two young sons who were now orphaned, and I wondered who would take care of them, and what would become of them. And then there was Joseph Stalin's death, which made us all feel better, even though we worried about who would take over the Communist leadership of Russia. Also, there was the truce that brought about the end of the Korean War. That made me very happy because it meant that my older brother, Paul, who was in the Army, would be coming home from South Korea soon, unscathed by the war.

When Angelo arrives with more newspapers I refill my bag, then walk up Quebec Road from the hospital and turn east down the northern side of Westwood Avenue. There I deliver papers down past Vitt and Stermer's Funeral Home, past my Aunt Carrie's house, past the rear of the convent house where the nuns who taught at St. Bonnies lived. I then proceed all the way down the next block, past my friend Billy Broxterman's new home, located next to the gas station on the northwest corner of Westwood and Grand, across the street from Shadwell Park. That's the end of my route. I leave my empty bag at the gas station for Angelo to pick up later, and then I walk home down Westwood until it merged with Harrison Avenue on the corner where the Spring Garden Building and Loan Bank stands.

Off to the right of that intersection is a one-lane street, an insignificant little road that leads from Westwood Avenue up to a small hill next to the railroad tracks, where it ends. Bald Knob rises on the other side of the tracks. The road hardly deserves the title of "Avenue," but there it is, Moellering Avenue, which is no more than twenty feet wide and 200 feet long. There are only three houses on the avenue, and ours is the first.

Next door to us is the house of Mr. and Mrs. Imm, and next to that is the last house, adjacent to the railroad tracks, where my childhood friends

Dick and Jerry Jung live. Strangely enough, our house has the address of 2225 Moellering Avenue. Why our address is not #1, I have no idea. My parents bought the house, and our family moved there from our apartment on Queen City Avenue in the Fall of 1942, shortly after my first birthday. Mom and Dad would continue to live there for over forty years until they both passed away in 1983.

By the time I reached home from delivering my papers I had walked at least three miles back and forth through the heart of South Fairmount (that's about a thousand miles a year!). I delivered over a hundred newspapers a day for about two years, and I was paid $4.75 a week, plus tips—not bad for a young kid in the early '50s. The tips I received, maybe a nickel or a dime here and there, at the most a quarter, came from the newspaper subscribers on my route.

Every second Saturday I'd knock on some of their doors to collect payment for the newspaper delivery. It wasn't the best part of my job, that's for sure, since most people would rather not see me show up to collect money from them. And for some reason I always seemed to knock on their doors at inappropriate times, and many of them would moan and complain as they fished through their wallets for a dollar or two to give me.

The worst part was collecting from the poor families that lived in the shabby tenements on Queen City Avenue across from the Shadwell Park swimming pool. These were the poorest of the poor, most of them recently arrived folks from Kentucky or West Virginia, whom we disparagingly called "the hillbillies." In July and August their third-floor apartment would be extremely hot, as hardly anyone in those days had that relatively new invention called air conditioning. Like many other families in South Fairmount, these poor folks just couldn't afford it. Some didn't even have enough money for electric fans.

The heat and the smell of cabbage soup boiling on the stove is suffocating as I step into the apartment. Two little kids with torn clothes, dirty faces and snotty noses run back and forth through the rooms. Their mother, a woman who is no more than 35 but who looks more like 60, appears to be losing her struggle to maintain the household. She approaches me with a sad smile that reveals a missing tooth or two, meekly apologizing that she doesn't have the money to pay for the papers. Yet she assures me that her husband would be home from work soon and maybe he could pay what they owe. That's fine with me, but I tell her I can't wait until then, so I leave.

Later, when I report to Angelo that I didn't collect their money, he looks at me as if I had failed him. I feel bad about it, but it's not my fault. He's upset, too, because he now has to climb the three floors and try to get them to pay. When they can't pay him, Angelo is stuck with the tab that he had to pay to the newspaper publisher. In return, he discontinues their newspaper delivery, which was good news to me, because I didn't want to climb up those hot and foul-smelling stairways anymore.

My newspaper route gave me an opportunity to see how the people of South Fairmount spent their lives, ranging from those families who were living on the edge of poverty, to those families who lived more comfortably and had the money to improve and decorate their homes and yards. All those days provided me with valuable lessons on how people lived and related to one another, lessons I would carry with me for the rest of my life. It was during those days that I became an observer of people and the ways they lived and the conversations they had. I believe that all that mental notetaking (although I wasn't even aware that I was taking notes) was what led to my later interest in theater and motion pictures, for each of the homes contained a wide variety of different characters and real-life dramas that were revealed to me on a daily basis.

I remember vividly those lovely sun-drenched June afternoons when I delivered my daily diet of words and pictures to my South Fairmount neighbors. Even now in my mind's eye I can see the C&O train crossing over the trestles high above Selim and Grand Avenues, and I can hear it hooting its greetings to the swimmers frolicking below in the Shadwell Park pool. Above us stands Bald Knob, a silent but friendly sentinel keeping watch over our valley.

During those days everything seemed beautiful and right with the world. It was then that I wished that South Fairmount would remain just like that forever, and if I could have stopped time and frozen that moment, I would have done so. But wish as I may, that was not to be. My childhood past now exists only in these memories I write seventy years later.

All these experiences, both positive and negative, planted in me a lasting love and nostalgia for South Fairmount, my home. For me, those were my "good old days," and they were also the final years of what I now believe was South Fairmount's Golden Age, those years just before things began to fall apart.

Actually, things had begun to change before the 1950s, but the transformation was rather slow and undetectable. By 1915 South Fairmount was a thriving community, but World War I, Prohibition, and the Great Depression began to bring about a dwindling population. With the rise of the automobile culture at the end of World War II, many of the middle-class families who could afford it began to move out of South Fairmount to the suburbs of Westwood, Cheviot, and beyond.

By the end of the 1950s it became clear that things were beginning to change more rapidly in South Fairmount, and by the middle 1960s buildings began to be torn down. Along with these changes there was an influx of poor people into the neighborhood. Many of them had been forced out of the blighted West End area of Cincinnati that had been undergoing urban renewal and the construction of Interstate 75. By 1965 South Fairmount's Golden Age was over. People and businesses began to move out, and today, sixty years later, it has become one of the most blighted neighborhoods in the city of Cincinnati.

Today, what was once my entire world, from the Western Hills Viaduct all the way west to Saint Francis Hospital, has been erased. Almost all of the houses on the south side of Queen City Avenue and the north side of Westwood Avenue, from Harrison Avenue in the east to Quebec Road to the west, have been demolished. That open area was cleared away for the "Lick Run Project," a plan by the city to improve the underground water and sewage system that drained the Western Hills, while at the same time replacing the lost homes with a scenic park and recreation area.

In a way, South Fairmount has once again, by the very name of the project, returned to its Lick Run roots. While the project may have been a necessary undertaking, it still saddens most of us who grew up in those golden days of South Fairmount, days that now exist only in the memories and photos we share with each other, as we lament the loss of our childhood and the passing of that wonderful moment in time.

8

INVISIBLE BOY

*I have been hurt to the point of abysmal
pain, hurt to the point of invisibility.*

Invisible Man
~ Ralph Ellison

When I was growing up nobody in my family recognized me. It pains me to say so, but that was the case—at least that's what I felt. As the fourth of six children and the youngest son, I was basically ignored and overlooked by parents who had six kids and were too busy with just getting food on the table and clothes on our backs to notice me. I had to fend for myself.

Being lost in the shuffle of daily life in a home where there were very few overt expressions of love and affection, I screamed silently for the recognition rarely given me, wanting so much to be heard and seen. But I rarely received any of that, and for the most part I felt ignored. At times I felt invisible. If that wasn't enough to be sad about, I also felt guilty and ashamed, for I came to believe that I was somehow responsible for the

Grupenhoff siblings, c. 1942. From left: John, Richard, Paul, Roseann.

condition in which I found myself. Loneliness, guilt and shame were three basic emotions that governed much of my behavior as a child.

One day early in 1950 my father told me that I'd be spending the next three weeks with my Aunt Carrie at her house on Westwood Avenue, which was located less than a hundred yards from Saint Bonnies. It was February, and since February's weather was often cold and wet, the thought of being able to walk to morning Mass and school in only two or three minutes was a welcomed one.

While packing up clothes for my stay, I thought to myself that I hadn't been told why I was to spend the next three weeks there. No explanations were given, and I was too afraid to ask for one. This inability to inquire about things that had an impact on my life reveals the level of fear I had of questioning my father's authority—or any authority, for that matter.

Even at that early age I'd already learned to do what I was told to do without being given a reason.

I soon settled into my new temporary home, sharing meals and evening radio shows with my mother's older sister, Aunt Carrie, and her husband, my uncle Theodore Vennemeyer, "Teets," as he was called. Uncle Teets was Saint Bonaventure's school custodian at the time, so he went to work at the same place I went to school. Now and then I'd pass him in the school's hallway, where he'd be pushing a wide dust mop. He smiled faintly and nodded to me as I passed, and I said hello in a whisper, feeling sorry for him because he seemed embarrassed to be seen this way by me, even though I felt proud of him.

By this time Uncle Teets and Aunt Carrie were in their fifties, and all their children but one had moved out of the house. Their youngest son, my cousin Frankie, who was about 20, was still there, but he had recently decided to become a monk at the Trappist monastery in Gethsemane, Kentucky, where he would spend the next 25 years in silence and celibacy as, ironically, "Brother Valentine." The day before he left he took me up to show me his bedroom where I would be sleeping during my stay, and while we were there he gave me a copy of Nordoff and Hall's novel, *Mutiny on the Bounty*, as a departing gift.

Every evening of my exile I'd read a chapter of the book before falling asleep. This was the first adult novel I ever read, and I became captivated by the story and its characters, especially the rebellious Fletcher Christian, whom I grew to admire, and the authoritarian Captain Bligh, whom I grew to detest. The colorful illustrations of bare-breasted Tahitian women also aroused my curiosity, although at eight years old I wasn't sure why. All I know is that my parents and the nuns would be very angry if they caught me looking at such "dirty" and "sinful" pictures of naked native women. To a young boy of eight, Tahiti seemed to be some unreachable, far-away exotic paradise, yet it seemed to beckon me to come. Someday, I thought, I will go there. (I finally did just that in August 2001, when my partner Carol Ann and I went to Tahiti to celebrate my 60th birthday.)

Time passed slowly at Aunt Carrie's, and after two weeks had gone by I had grown lonely and very homesick, so one sunny Saturday afternoon I decided to walk a mile back home to see what was happening there. I approached my house with some anxiety, since I had decided to visit without letting anyone know I was coming. When I walked through the front door my father was sitting in the living room listening to the radio and smoking a cigar. When he saw me he seemed both surprised and annoyed. He sprang up out of his chair and barked at me, "What are you doing here?" Taken aback, I meekly responded, "Well, this is my home, isn't it?"

Though clearly upset by my surprise appearance, Dad couldn't deny my response, and he relented. "OK, come with me. I have something to show you." He ushered me into the next room, and there was my mother in bed, coddling a new baby. "Here's your new little sister," Dad said, "her name is Joyce." Then he abruptly turned and left the room. He displayed neither pride nor happiness about being a new father for the sixth time, and he showed little consideration for either Mom or Joyce. More than anything, he seemed embarrassed.

But Mom was happy to see me, and she smiled at me and introduced me to Joyce, who was now about a week old. I sat on the edge of the bed with Joyce's little hand wrapped around my finger. I was neither happy nor sad, just surprised and confused as to why this had happened and why I hadn't been told about it. Yet, in my fear I was unable to articulate the simple question, "Why?" I felt like a stranger in my own home.

After I had spent about five minutes with Mom and Joyce, Dad returned and said, "OK, I think it's time for you to leave." I grew annoyed because he was pushing me away once again. But I wanted to stay as long as possible, so I fabricated a lie.

"May I go up to my bedroom first? I want to get a book off the shelf to take with me." I surprised myself by that response, for it was the first time I can remember lying to my father face-to-face.

Dad said yes, and I went up to my attic bedroom, wishing more than anything that I could sleep there that night (and every night thereafter). Tears welled up in my eyes as I stood looking out the window at our back yard and up to the railroad tracks that separated our house from the base of Bald Knob. My own father was expelling me, once again, from the only home I had ever known.

After a minute or two, Dad opened the door at the bottom of the steps and yelled for me to hurry up. I said okay, but before I went back down I laid down on my bed for a few moments, just to recall how familiar and pleasant it felt. Then I got up and picked a random book off the shelf to cover my lie, and when I went downstairs I passed once more through my parents' bedroom. Mom, obviously annoyed by Dad's behavior and sympathetic to my plight, whispered, "Are you hungry?" I nodded yes. "Then, before you leave," she said, "go to the kitchen and make yourself a liverwurst sandwich and a glass of milk."

She knew that that was one of my favorite snacks, so I went into the kitchen and spread Miracle Whip thickly onto two pieces of Wonder Bread and placed two slices of liverwurst between them and then cut the sandwich diagonally, as Mom had taught me, creating two triangles, so I could eat it more elegantly, "Like the rich people do," she would say.

I sat alone at the kitchen table beneath the Hudepohl Beer sign on the wall that had a clock face on it, watching the second hand ticking off moment by moment, one after the other. I silently ate my sandwich as elegantly as I could, and I drank the milk as slowly as possible. But soon Dad came to the kitchen doorway and pestered me once more to leave.

He really doesn't like me, I thought. But by that time I was so annoyed by his persistence that I wanted to leave. So I finished eating, got up, deliberately left the book I had taken from my bedroom on the table, and said goodbye to Mom and Joyce – but not to Dad. I left home, resenting my new-born sister Joyce for getting me kicked out of the house once again, detesting my father for how he had treated me, and feeling very sad and angry as I trudged back to Aunt Carrie's house.

This was such a traumatic experience for me that I repressed the memory of it. I didn't recall it again until I was in psychoanalysis over forty years later. The memory of that event suddenly bubbled up from my unconscious. Its recollection was a liberating moment, permitting me to understand more clearly my difficult relationship with my father.

That breakthrough had also given me an insight into my family's sexual repression and their inability to tell me that a new baby was on the way. Although I now realize that I had been sent to live with my aunt and uncle because there was so much to do at home that I would probably just get in the way, I still don't understand why I was told to do this without knowing the reason.

Nobody had explained to me in the months leading up to my sister's birth that my mother was going to have another baby. Of course, in those days nothing concerning sex was ever discussed in our house and, since my mother was fairly heavy to begin with, I never really noticed that she was pregnant. Later I discovered that I was the only one in my family that was kept in the dark about the new baby. And when I was sent off to Aunt Carrie's, I literally became that invisible boy my father apparently wanted me to be.

My time in analysis led me to realize that I had, at best, a love/hate relationship with my father. As far as I can remember, he never taught me anything, never encouraged me in any endeavor, never asked me my future plans, never indicated how I might be successful at something, and never once simply told me that he loved me. Recognition, encouragement, love—these were the things I craved the most, but these cravings were rarely, if ever, fulfilled.

My earliest memories of my father were that he seemed psychologically distant from me, and at times I felt he resented me for simply being born, and that he didn't care about my problems. Every time I asked him for help or to do something for me, he seemed to feel it was an intrusion or a burden for him, and when he did do something it was usually because my mother pressured him to do it.

After a while, I simply stopped asking. We joked around now and then, and I enjoyed his verbal wordplay and bad jokes. Yet, there were no positive feelings from him towards me that I could detect, no emotional displays of affection, never hugs nor applause—just criticism, mostly. He provided no guidance or structure—in short, none of those supportive things that help a young boy build a healthy ego and provide him with a measure of confidence and self-esteem. And having received neither attention nor affection, I grew incapable of giving any.

No one taught me how to face the people and problems I would meet in the years to come. Love was a mere mirage that they only talked about in the movies, and the concepts of love and happiness in my life had no meaning for me. So, what I did was to internalize my loneliness and my fear that no one really cared about me. My defense was to build psychological walls designed to keep pain away—not only physical pain, but emotional pain as well.

When I wanted to avoid something, or make it stop, I would simply close my eyes until it was gone. I would shut it off, or walk away, or go to bed with the blankets over my head. In short, I became invisible. My world narrowed, and I only paid attention, through my instinct, to my day-to-day survival. I wanted so much to be able to reach out and touch another soul, yet I was still unable to love because I was never taught how to love.

Even my grade school "puppy loves" were eventually disappointing, because once I experienced positive feelings about a girl, I didn't know what to do next. I didn't know how to express care and concern, and so those early relationships faded within a few days, most likely because the girls thought me rather boring, and I can't blame them for that, since it was probably true. It was only during my teen-age years that I began to throw off some of my fears and doubts, probably because hanging out with my high-school friends stimulated in me some self-awareness and confidence in myself that I never received at home.

9

SHADWELL PARK

Play is the work of childhood.

~ Mr. Rogers

When I was growing up much of my free time in the summers was spent roaming around my neighborhood on Queen City and Westwood Avenues. From about 1947 to 1955 I spent much of that time at Shadwell Park, bordered by those two streets and Grand Avenue. Originally part of the lowlands that the old Lick Run stream carved through the valley, Shadwell Park became the center of recreational activity in South Fairmount.

Every two or three years the park flooded, especially in springtime, when the March and April rains soaked the western hills, and the underground sewers couldn't handle the volume of water that came flowing down. In some years the flooding would start at Grand Avenue and stretch down Shadwell Park and out through the narrow alley behind Kroger's and the West Hills Theater all the way down to Harrison Avenue, eventually spilling into the Mill Creek.

Constructed in the early 1930s, Shadwell Park contained two baseball fields, tennis courts, swings, muscle bars and sandboxes. But its main feature during the summer was the city-run public swimming pool. The water in the main pool was only about four feet at the deepest end, and there was a separate wading pool for small children and toddlers.

I often spent two or three afternoons a week at the pool in the summers during those years. My friends and I would pack sandwiches and a few cookies in a small brown paper bag and walk to the pool in our gym shoes and bathing suits with our towels wrapped around our necks and shoulders, and sometimes we would run towards the park with our towels billowing in the wind, pretending we were Superman.

Because so many kids crowded into the pool we often had to have special hours for different ages, and I can remember having a boys' hour and a girls' hour, too. When it was the girls' hour to swim the boys would go out onto the grass area between the pool and the tennis courts to eat lunch. Then we would slather our bodies with baby lotion to get a good suntan, but all I usually got was a sunburn that would be so bad that in a few days my chest and back would develop blisters that would ultimately dry up and become flakey, and I would then peel off pieces of skin as big as half-dollars. More than once we had contests to see who could get the best sunburn. If you didn't at least get blisters you were a wimp. In those days we had no concept of skin cancer, and no one had ever heard of melanoma.

But the pool wasn't only used for recreational swimming. On holiday weekends we would have swimming races and other contests. My favorite was the watermelon contest, usually held around the Fourth of July. Two teams of about five on each side would vie to capture the watermelon, which was covered in oil or lard and then tossed into the center of the pool. The contest, something of a no-holds-barred combination of water polo and rugby, would be won by the first team to get the slippery watermelon and carry it to their end of the pool. It sounds like it might be easy, but hanging onto the greased watermelon was quite difficult, especially when your opponents were trying to grab you or grab the watermelon from you. Sometimes the contest would last a good fifteen minutes before there was a victory, and the struggle between the teams was always both furious and hilarious.

At least once a week in the evenings the pool was closed for cleaning and drained of water, and we'd play dodgeball inside the empty pool until sundown. It was a perfect arena for dodgeball. Everyone who was in the game had to stay inside the empty pool. If you were hit and eliminated, you had to get out. The unique part of the game was that, if you threw the ball at another player and missed, the ball might hit the inner side of the pool and bounce right back to you, so you could throw it again.

There was no age limit to play the game, and we often had nine- and ten-year-old kids playing against 13- and 14-year-olds. The older kids let the young ones play because the little kids were considered easy marks, and most of them would be eliminated early in the game. But sometimes the young ones would hang back and not get involved, running back and forth in the pool away from the ball. That way, after some of the older kids had been eliminated, some of the young kids were still in the game, but I don't remember any of them ever winning.

I didn't realize it at the time, but the baseball field at Shadwell was the site of my first brush with greatness. I was ten years old in the Spring of 1952, and I was on the field trying out for the Knot Hole League baseball team managed by Pep Neumann. In order to make the team, a player had to be given a contract, which was basically an insurance waiver. It was a Friday, and there was only one contract remaining to be handed out. The year before I had been a catcher for the team, but this year a new kid, Chuck Garnett, moved into our neighborhood, and he beat me out for that position.

Looking for another position to play, I began taking grounders on the infield. Just then another kid who I had never seen before came out onto the diamond and started taking grounders at second base. It only took a few ground balls for me to realize this kid was better than me—and better than anyone else on the team, for that matter. I went home that night convinced that I would not make the team, and that this new kid would get the final contract. I basically told myself that things were hopeless, and that there was no reason for me to return tomorrow for the final day of tryouts.

But the next day I decided to go to the field anyway, though I don't remember what it was that changed my mind. When I got to the park I noticed that the new kid wasn't there, and after tryouts I was given the last contract. I made the team! Surprised by my good fortune, I asked my friend Jerry, whose father managed the team, what happened to that kid who was out here yesterday.

"Who are you talking about?" Jerry asked.

Now, most of the kids in our neighborhood came from German families, and their last names, like mine, were easily recognized as such, so I would have never remembered this kid's name unless it was so different—which it definitely was.

"You know," I said, "that kid who came out yesterday and was fielding ground balls. I think your dad called him Pete."

Oh," said Jerry, "you're talking about Pete Rose. His dad is a friend of my dad, and they just came down for a visit. They live in Sedamsville, so Pete lives outside our district, and he has to play for another team."

And that's the story of how I, a mediocre ballplayer at best, beat Pete Rose out for our Little League team—on a technicality, of course!

In April 1963 I was a freshman at Xavier University. I had just walked into the South Hall cafeteria on campus when I glanced up at the black and white TV above the food counter. It was opening day for the Cincinnati Reds, and I was shocked when they introduced their new rookie, a kid by the name of Pete Rose! I joined my frends at one of the tables and told them that I had beaten Pete out for my Little League team years before, but they only laughed at me and scoffed at such a claim.

Pete Rose would eventually become the National League's Rookie of the Year for 1963, and later he finished his Major League career with the most hits in baseball history—more than Ty Cobb, Hank Aaron or Stan Musial. Yet he's still not in the Hall of Fame! But that's another story.

10

MY LIFE WITH THE BOOGIE MAN

The Boogie Man will get you if you don't watch out!
~ Sinbad, An Operatic Extravaganza

The first time I saw a black man was in the late 1940s, shortly after World War II. I was playing on the iron guard railings in the front of the Spring Garden Building and Loan Bank at the intersection of Westwood and Harrison Avenues when, out of nowhere, an elderly black man wearing threadbare clothes and a weathered fedora with holes in it drove past me in a cart drawn by a mangy-looking mule. The man was shouting out "Rag Man!" to all the housewives in the neighborhood. His business was to collect all the rags, old clothing and other junk they no longer wanted.

I was no more than six or seven years old, and I was fascinated by the sight of him as he drove his cart up Westwood Avenue. Where did he come from? And where did he go when he left our neighborhood? Did he have a home? And did he have a family? When I asked these questions I was told to steer clear of him, because he might be the Boogie Man who would kidnap me and throw me in his sack, and I would never see my family and neighborhood again. This was my initiation into prejudice and racial stereotyping. And so, at that early age, like many other children in my neighborhood, I was indoctrinated with the idea that black men were to be avoided, because they might be evil, although deep down I never really believed it.

In those days just after the war and before the Civil Rights Movement, nobody referred to such a person as "black." They were "Colored" or "Negroes," but it was also quite common for them to be called the derisive "N-word." Still, I felt sorry for the rag man, for he seemed to be a gentle soul living on the edge of poverty, and I didn't believe he could be an evil Boogie Man.

During my grade-school years I rarely saw a black person. I don't recall any black kids in Saint Bonnies school. By the time I was eight or nine rumors began to spread about Negroes coming to live in our neighborhood, and many seemed quite upset about that possibility. However, one day in the early 1950s it finally happened: the first black family moved into South Fairmount. And they moved into, of all places, the house next door to us! An elderly couple, Mr. and Mrs. Imm, had lived in that house for years, but they had recently moved away, and the house went up for sale, and somehow the real estate agent was able to move the black family in. That was the beginning of racial integration in South Fairmount.

Shortly after the black family moved in next door a chilling event occurred. It was late at night, and I was in bed asleep when people talking loudly downstairs startled me awake, and I got up to find out what was happening. My sister Roseann had just returned from being out with her friends. It was about 10 p.m. when she got in, and she noticed that a large white cross about six feet high had been planted on our front lawn. Realizing what had happened, Dad called the police, who soon arrived with a man who identified himself as an FBI agent. The agent explained to us that this cross was the work of the Ku Klux Klan, meant to terrorize the new family next door, but they apparently erected the cross in front of the wrong house. They might have set the cross on fire, had not Roseann arrived when she did. We were lucky, the FBI agent said, since the KKK could have mistakenly burned our house down with all of us inside.

I was stunned by this revelation, and I realized, even at that young age, that the problems of race had a negative effect on both blacks and whites. But most of all I felt empathy for all black people who had been the victims of racism. I felt they were no better or worse than any other human being, and they should not have to suffer prejudice and ostracism because of the color of their skin.

There were only a handful of young black students at Roger Bacon High School in the late 1950s, and when I joined the Navy in 1959 almost all the sailors were white. In boot camp, my company of 70 recruits had only two black men in it. Even though President Truman had integrated the armed forces in 1948, apparently the Navy had been slow to react. The only blacks I rarely saw were the cooks and valets who comprised the officers' mess-hall staff. None were on the deck force or served in any other capacity, and none of them slept or showered in the same compartments as the rest of the crew. It remained that way, at least on my ship, until I was discharged in 1962.

One of the first part-time jobs I took when I got out of the Navy and began college was that of a credit insurance investigator, one who scrutinized the backgrounds of those who had applied for life or auto insurance. I'd have a list of questions to ask neighbors and employers about the character of the applicant, questions such as: Was he a sober man? Did he have a regular job? Was he a responsible parent? Was he a reliable employee?

After I had interviewed two or three informants I filled out a report and recommended whether the applicant should be given the insurance or not. I didn't care much for the idea that I was investigating the private lives of people, and rarely did I recommend that a person to be turned down for insurance, no matter what questionable behavior I discovered about them.

One of my cases concerned a violinist for the Cincinnati Orchestra who was about 70 years old and was applying for auto insurance. My investigation found that he drove a red Corvette convertible, and he was often seen escorting different women out on dates. I approved him. My boss, however, came back to me and said, "We can't approve this man."

"Why not?" I asked.

"Well, he's seventy years old and he might have a heart attack while speeding down the road in his convertible. And he's living a wild life!" my boss said.

"He's an artist," I responded.

"Exactly," he said. "Case closed!"

Because I was taking classes in college my work hours were staggered. I usually got into the office after my last class around two in the afternoon, but by that time most of the cases had been taken by the regular salaried employees, and I was left with "the bottom of the barrel." Which meant I got the cases that were in the worst part of the city. Which also meant that I got most of the black applications to investigate, the ones no one else in the office wanted.

Much of my time during the year or so that I worked there was spent dealing with cases in the West End of Cincinnati, where many of the black families lived. The funny thing was that I didn't mind going there so much, maybe because I was simply too naive, or perhaps because I grew up rather poor, so I understood some of what these folks were going through. Nor did I feel frightened or intimidated as I walked through the all-black neighborhood, going door-to-door gathering information about the applicants.

Still, many of the informants were reluctant to talk to a white man in a sport coat and tie about the quality of their neighbors' lives, and I could understand that. Mine wasn't an enviable position to be in, and there were numerous times when I was rebuffed, and I had to leave without gathering any new information.

But now and then I would knock on a door, and someone would open it and allow me in. Once I happened upon an older woman giving a "process" hairdo to a younger one, and the licorice smell of the processing chemicals stung my nostrils. Inside the apartment the atmosphere was thick and oppressive. There was no air conditioning, and only a fan or two gave minimal relief from the heat.

I introduced myself and showed my credentials and asked, "Is this the home of James Smith?"

"No," the older woman said. I could tell immediately that she was trying to protect him from me, this white intruder.

"Well, on his application for auto insurance, James Smith gives this as his home address. Does he live here?" I asked.

"Oh, you must mean Jimmy Smith! Yeah, he lives here. He's my brother. We never call him James, so that is why I didn't understand who you meant," she said. After she answered a few more questions I thanked her and said goodbye. Back at the office, I filed my report and recommended James Smith for the auto insurance.

The West End was my education in what it was like living at the lower rungs of society in Cincinnati in 1963. I learned more about life that year than I did in my formal classes at Xavier University. As I walked the streets around Central Avenue and Linn Street I came to view and understand the oppression black people had to put up with in Cincinnati, and how they were treated with a mixture of condescension, pity, fear and distrust by many white people. Even one hundred years after a Civil War that was fought to end slavery, blacks were still considered second-class citizens in a country that professed that all men were equal. I witnessed how they had to scratch out their meager existence, hoping to escape poverty and prejudice, and if not, then at least hoping that their sons and daughters might finally escape and get a decent education and a good job and join the middle class.

That hope was stirred by the Civil Rights Movement that began in the 1950s, and was later spearheaded by Dr. Martin Luther King, Jr., who's "I Have a Dream" speech at the "March on Washington" rally in 1963 called for equality for all African Americans. It remains for me the greatest speech I've ever heard, and it galvanized my spirit to fight for equal civil rights of all oppressed classes. It was on the streets of Cincinnati that I realized that, although I was not of the same skin color, I was someone who empathized with their pain and suffering, and I joined in solidarity with their struggle for equality.

While in graduate school at Ohio State University I participated in many Civil Rights demonstrations and anti-Vietnam War protests, which eventually became linked because of the large number of blacks who were being sent to Vietnam to fight a needless war. Muhammad Ali, the great boxing champion, had refused to be inducted into the Army to fight in Vietnam, and was stripped of his title and sent to prison. His heroic stance as a conscientious objector endeared him to blacks, sympathetic whites, and the emerging counter-culture generation.

Twenty years later in 1983, when I was a university professor, I assigned my film production students to make a short documentary film about black cowboys in Philadelphia, an experience which, by a strange confluence of events, led me to meet and write the biography of Lorenzo

Tucker, an early film actor once known as "The Colored Valentino." My interviews with him, and my research led me to become a scholar and historian of African American theatre and film, from the black-faced minstrel shows of the 1800s to the "Race Movies" that blacks produced from the 1920s until the 1950s.

Much of my scholarly work required me to do research at the New York Public Library's Schomburg Center for Research on Black Culture, located in Harlem on 135th Street. I also met and interviewed elderly black actors and producers, including Dick Campbell, himself an important figure in the history of black entertainment in America, who had known and worked with Lorenzo Tucker. I grew comfortable walking the streets of Harlem, even though I was at times the only white man on the street, and I felt no anxiety or fear. I accepted these people for who they were, and I believe they accepted me. They were normal people with the same hopes and desires I shared, and to this day I continue to work on behalf of achieving equality for all.

As a result of my research on Lorenzo Tucker, my book and articles were recognized as pioneering scholarship in the field. That recognition led to numerous speaking engagements and lectures at such universities as Harvard and Columbia. I am also happy that I had the opportunity to lecture on the topic at the University of Osnabrück, and I hoped that the spirits of my ancestors would be pleased with my return. And later I lectured on Race Movies at my Alma Mater, Xavier University, in 2017, fifty-one years after I had graduated from there. I also taught a course in African American Independent Film History every year for more than twenty years at Rowan University.

So, this is my story of living with the Boogie Man, who, it turns out, was a white man who has a long and fascinating history that stretches back centuries to the folklore and fairy tales of Europe, although in my childhood he was always black. The irony is that the song I quoted at the beginning of this chapter was first written in 1891 for an operatic extravaganza entitled *Sinbad*. The Boogie Man was white, and was there to scare the little black children:

> *Come all my little cannibals, and listen to me,*
> *A creature very strange is calling o'er the sea....*
> *Here comes the Boogie Man, he'll catch you if he can,*
> *A white man you have never seen, since first your lives began,*
> *No wonder when you see him you will call him the Boogie Man.*

11

THE SAILBOAT

*I would prefer even to fail with
honor than win by cheating.*

~ Sophocles

One Friday around 1952 Dad brought home a model sailboat. It was about two feet long with a white sail almost two feet high. It was a beauty. The sailboat was to be given as a prize at the games that were to be held that coming Sunday at Saint Bonnies' summer festival, and my father was in charge of getting some of the prizes together. Dad said that the competition for my age group (I was nine), would be to push a peanut shell with our noses about twenty feet. The first boy to cross the finish line would be awarded the sailboat.

For two days the sailboat was stored in the corner of our dining room, surrounded by other prizes that were to be awarded at the games, and even though I wasn't allowed to touch the boat, I sat there Saturday morning with my eyes glued to it, coveting it for hours. I desired it so much that I decided that my goal would be to finish first and win the sailboat, and so I spent Saturday afternoon practicing by pushing a peanut shell back and forth across our kitchen floor until my knees became raw and sore.

I didn't have a lake or pond nearby to sail the boat, but that didn't matter. I would have been happy just to sit in my bedroom every night and admire the boat before I turned off the lights and fell asleep, hoping I would dream that I was on the boat sailing to some exotic land, like Tahiti.

It seemed to take forever for Sunday to arrive, and when I went to Mass that morning I prayed to the Blessed Virgin to help me win the sailboat, and when I left church I was confident she would. My friends and I took the shuttle bus from the church to the fairgrounds where the festival was being held. It was a warm sunny Sunday afternoon in August as we walked down the main concourse between rows of booths and tents that housed games of chance like the Big Six and the Kentucky Derby, where for a quarter you could bet on a horse, like Man o' War or Whirlaway, and hope the spinning wheel would make you a winner. Other booths sold beer, and some sold foods like corn-on-the-cob, cotton candy, or bratwursts slathered with mustard and topped with steaming sauerkraut. As I passed by the booths I promised myself that I would come back and buy a bratwurst and a Coke to celebrate my sailboat victory.

But for now, I headed to the area where the games were being held. I passed the egg-throwing contest for the older men, and the three-legged races for the teenagers. I stopped to watch them for a moment, then hurried to the picnic shelter, where the contests for the children were being held. While I watched a contest for the younger kids I wrapped my knees with two handkerchiefs I had brought from home to ease the pain I would suffer from crawling on the cement floor.

Finally, it was peanut-pushing time! As we knelt down at the starting line, I overheard one of the kids next to me tell his friend that he was going to blow the peanut while he was pushing it with his nose. "I'll get a few more inches each time," he said gleefully. Immediately I became distressed by his statement, and I thought to myself, "Nobody's going to cheat me out of the sailboat, and if he's going to cheat like that, then so am I."

Suddenly the starter's whistle blew, and the race was on! At first I fell behind, but then I began to blow the peanut after each nudge with my nose, and before I knew it the race was over, and I had won—Mary had answered my prayers! The judge overseeing the race, however, had observed me cheating, and pointed it out to the crowd watching, and instead of awarding me the sailboat, he gave it to the second-place finisher–the very boy who said at the starting line that he was going to cheat!

Of course, I was mortified, and I knew I deserved the punishment. I had sacrificed my honor in order to win by cheating.

But there is more to this story: the judge who disqualified me was none other than my own father, who should have known to remove himself as judge prior the race, since his own son was participating in it. That would also have saved him the embarrassment of having to publicly point out to the spectators that his own son was a cheater.

Publicly denounced and humiliated by my father, I shamefully walked away from him and my friends, who probably didn't want anything to do with me anyway. When I was out of their sight I rushed back through the main concourse, running past the booths and not even stopping to buy a bratwurst and a Coke—there would be no sailboat celebration today. I then climbed aboard the shuttle bus that was getting ready to return to the church. I had to get out of there. I was alone, filled with shame and self-loathing, and I sat in silence during the ride back, anguished that I had failed the Blessed Virgin, persuaded I was a cheater and a sinner, and convinced that I would never amount to anything of any value.

In the following days there was only silence. My father never said a word to me about the incident, never asked me why I cheated, never asked me how I felt about it, never told me how he felt about it, never attempted to console me about the loss of the sailboat, and never sat me down to talk to me about it and turn the event into a teachable moment. But I did learn two things: first, from that day forward I never cheated in games or contests I participated in; second, and most importantly, I learned that my father was practically incapable of relating to me, or of understanding my feelings. He was not someone I could turn to for help or advice, for he had none to give me.

12

MY LIFE IN THE MOVIES

*Movies touch our heart and awaken our
vision, and change the way we see things.*

~ Martin Scorsese

On Saturday afternoons in the early 1950s I would meet my friends at the West Hills Theater on Queen City Avenue to watch the movie matinee. The West Hills was a small neighborhood theater in South Fairmount, with about 400 seats at most, but in the late 1940s and early '50s it was my childhood kingdom of dreams. It was also a classroom, a place where I sat in the darkness and learned about the lives of other human beings, about their hopes, their needs and desires, their joys and suffering, and about what drives them to do what they choose to do. It was there in the darkness that I took my first philosophy and sociology courses. That might sound strange, but I do know that I learned more about life through the movies than I learned in school.

Some of the movies I remember seeing were *Bambi, The Adventures of Robin Hood, The Sands of Iwo Jima, The Jim Thorpe Story, The Sea Hawk, Battleground, Steel Helmet, High Noon, Singin' in the Rain, Viva Zapata,*

On the Waterfront, Rock Around the Clock, Stalag 17, Shane, The Glenn Miller Story, The Egyptian, The Thing, Rear Window, Rebel Without a Cause, The Wild One, and *Blackboard Jungle.* These films, and many more that I can no longer recall, were not only entertaining, but they also helped me shape the values and standards that would guide my life. All these movies had a powerful emotional effect on me, and I believe that's why I remember them.

I went to my first movie when I was very young, probably about six years old. Although memories had not established a firm foothold in my mind at that age, I do recall that at my earliest movie experience I encountered the concept of death for the first time. It happened around 1948 when my older sister, Roseann, took me to the movies one sunny Saturday. When we rounded the corner we discovered a long line of people stretching down the sidewalk, waiting to enter the theater for the matinee screening of Walt Disney's *Bambi*. I remember little else except for the long wait in line and the crush of the crowd and the rush for decent seats before someone else would get to them.

I watched *Bambi* wide-eyed, captivated by the animation and by the story of a young deer growing to maturity after he had lost his mother, who had been killed by human hunters. When the movie was over I left the theater and the sunlight hit my eyes and I had to squint for the next few minutes while my eyes adjusted to the light. At the same time, tears were running down my cheeks, because *Bambi* had given me my first encounter with the idea of death. The movie taught me that parents die, and in that moment it dawned on me that sooner or later my parents would also die. That's why I was crying. (Years later I read where the novelist Stephen King said that *Bambi* was the first horror movie he ever saw. I agree with him!)

* * * * *

Thirty-five years later, in September 1983, I received a call from my brother John, telling me that our father, who was 75 years old, had a stroke and was now in a coma, and there was no chance of recovery. Just the night before I had been out to the Moshulu Restaurant in Philadelphia with my wife, Carolyn, my older brother John and his wife, Suzanne, and Mom and Dad. We were celebrating dual birthdays—John and I were born on the same day, seven years apart. It was a pleasant night for celebrating our shared birthday, even though John and I got into a rather heated discussion about the new AIDS epidemic and homosexuals.

Dad was sitting across from me, and I noticed that his face seemed rather bloated and ashen. He appeared tired and rarely talked to any of us during the meal, and he obviously wasn't interested in eating the rare-cooked steak bleeding on the plate in front of him. Of course, I had no idea then that this would be the final dinner I would ever have with him and, even more alarming, that this would be the final dinner of his life. The last time I saw him alive was after the meal when he got into the back seat of John's car, and I shook his hand and said goodbye. The next morning he suffered his fatal stroke at John's house in Maryland.

I don't remember much of the telephone conversation with John when he informed me of Dad's stroke and impending death. Nor do I remember hanging up the phone. The next thing I recall was that I was out in my backyard kicking a tree in anger. I must have been upset with Nature for taking my father away from me. As I kicked the tree, I suddenly thought once again—for the first time in almost forty years—of *Bambi*, and of how I cried when Bambi lost his parents. I had repressed that negative emotional reaction to *Bambi* deep in my unconscious, but my father's death triggered that memory back into my consciousness. This is a good example of how the emotional power of the movies can have a lasting impact upon someone, even after decades.

* * * * *

The Jim Thorpe Story (1951) made a huge impression on me, even though I was only 10 years old. It helped shape my feelings about prejudice and how our culture mistreated racial minorities, in this case Native Americans. I had seen many westerns where the cowboys defeated the hated "injuns" like Geronimo. But when I saw this film I began to understand the long history of genocide and pain the white man inflicted on Native Americans.

I became angry when the film revealed that the U.S. Olympics committee stripped Jim Thorpe of the gold medals he won at the 1912 Olympics. They discovered he had played some games with a semi-pro baseball team before the Olympics and got paid for it, which was against the rules. The fact that he was paid made him, according to the committee, a professional, and professional athletes were not permitted at that time to compete in the Olympics, which was open only to amateurs.

But even then, as young as I was, I understood that the unspoken reason they stripped him of his medals was because he was a Native American, not a white man. Happily, in 1983 the International Olympics Committee partially reversed their earlier decision and restored Jim Thorpe's medals. Only recently, in 2022, did the Committee restore his full reputation by indicating he was the sole winner of the events he participated in.

Burt Lancaster portrayed Jim Thorpe in the film, and over the years he became one of my favorite actors. I've always thought that he, more than any other male actor during Hollywood's Golden Age, had the most intense and powerful presence on the screen. In his 1960 film, *Elmer Gantry*, he played a preacher/con man with such intensity that his performance garnered him the Academy Award for Best Actor.

I couldn't predict then that in 1979 I would be on the Boardwalk in Atlantic City, watching Lancaster act during the production of the film *Atlantic*

City, but that is exactly what happened. I took my film production class down to Atlantic City to watch some of the exterior scenes being filmed. In one of the scenes we watched, Lancaster was talking with a drug dealer while walking a little dog on a leash. He and the drug dealer were having a conversation when all of a sudden the dog stopped and refused to go further. Lancaster pulled on the leash, but the dog wouldn't budge. They tried shooting the scene a second time, but when the dog got to the same spot he froze again. He wouldn't move. The assistant director called for the dog's stand-in, or back-up.

Surprised, I asked myself, do movie dogs have stand-ins? Well, this one did, and within minutes they were ready to reshoot the scene with the new dog. The director called "Action," and the characters began to walk down the boardwalk. Then, at exactly the same place the first dog froze, this dog did, too! The director shouted "Cut!" and, obviously frustrated, ran over to Lancaster. What were they going to do? Change the location?

"Don't worry," Lancaster said. "I'll take care of it. Let's do one more take."

The crew re-set and began the shot. As the actors walked down the boardwalk they got to the point where both dogs froze, and the second dog did it again. Without missing a beat, Lancaster bent down and picked up the little dog and cradled it in his arms and they continued to walk down the boardwalk and complete the scene. I stood there in awe as I watched him save the scene. It was a small but beautiful moment of improvisation that any actor could learn from.

The director of the Jim Thorpe movie was Michael Curtiz. I didn't realize it at the time, but Curtiz had also directed another of my favorite movies, *The Adventures of Robin Hood* (1938), starring Errol Flynn and Basil Rathbone. Curtiz was one of the great studio directors during Hollywood's Golden Age. He directed Errol Flynn in *Captain Blood* (1935), the film that made Flynn a star. He also directed Cincinnati native Doris Day in her first movie, *Romance on the High Seas*, in 1948. Over the years Curtiz directed Humphrey Bogart and Ingrid Bergman in *Casablanca*, Kirk Douglas in *Young Man with a Horn*, Joan Crawford in *Mildred Pierce*, and Elvis Presley in *King Creole*. His greatest accomplishment was directing one of America's most loved movies, *Casablanca*, for which he won the Academy Award.

By 1964 I was the entertainment columnist for my college newspaper, the *Xavier News*, and I conducted my first celebrity interview with Basil Rathbone, who had played the evil Sir Guy in *The Adventures of Robin Hood*, where he had that incredible sword fight with Errol Flynn that ended in Sir Guy's death. He was probably more famous, however, for his recurring role as Sherlock Holmes in a series of films from the 1930s and '40s. When I met him he was 72 years old, and he was on a one-man tour of his show, "In and Out of Character," which was also the title of his autobiography. He appeared in Cincinnati at Mount Saint Joseph College. His program featured soliloquies from Shakespeare's plays, along with humorous anecdotes from his life and career.

I interviewed him in his dressing room backstage just before the show. When the stage manager called for him, he asked me to join him, and we walked from the dressing room to the backstage wings. A minute before he was to go on stage he asked the stage manager to bring him a piece of wood. The stage manager brought him a two-by-four about a foot long. Basil took it and immediately rapped his knuckles on it.

"Can't go on without knocking on wood," he grinned at me, almost apologetically. I thought it strange that such a sophisticated and worldly-wise artist should find it necessary to rely on this old theatrical superstition. Yet, in keeping with tradition, I whispered "Break a leg," to him, and he smiled at me once more and then walked out onto the stage. That was the last I spoke with him. Three years later he passed away.

At the West Hills I also saw some great war movies, including *The Sands of Iwo Jima*, *Steel Helmet* and *Battleground*. After watching these films, my friends and I would stage our own battle scenes in the ashes and slag piles in the dump behind the Twin Trolleys restaurant across from the Lunkenheimer valve plant at the corner of Queen City and Beekman Avenues. We spent hours throwing fake hand grenades at Nazi machine-gun nests and scouring Japanese bunkers with our imaginary flamethrowers. On those hot summer afternoons we thought our battles were even greater than the Normandy invasion!

Near the top of my list of favorite films when I was a kid was *Stalag 17*. Rarely did I have the money to see a movie more than once, but I must have seen *Stalag 17* at least four or five times, always waiting for that hilarious scene when Robert Strauss and Harvey Lembeck begin painting a stripe down the middle of the road, passing the German guards, hoping to get to the Russian women prisoners' barracks. These days I am reminded of that movie when I watch late-night TV re-runs of "Hogan's Heroes," the 1960's comedy TV series modeled after *Stalag 17*.

The director of *Stalag 17* was Billy Wilder, and I had no idea then who he was. It was only later when I began to study film history that I came to realize that he was one of the greatest writers and directors Hollywood ever produced, having won six Academy Awards during his career. A refugee who fled from Nazi Germany, he directed his first film in Hollywood, *Double Indemnity*, in 1944, which is now considered one of the best *film noirs* ever made. And his gender-bending *Some Like It Hot* (1959) is often considered Hollywood's #1 all-time romantic comedy.

The first time I saw *On the Waterfront* I was about 12 or 13, and I was absolutely captivated and astonished by it. A young and thin Marlon Brando, arguably the greatest American actor of the second half of the 20thCentury, was brilliant as Terry Malloy, of course, but equally as intriguing to me was the performance of Karl Malden, who played the waterfront priest. His redemptive speech about Christ being there among the stevedores in the hold of the ship brought tears to my eyes and choked me up for the next ten minutes. And the priest drank beer and smoked cigarettes! That was mind-boggling to me, a young Catholic boy who once considered becoming a priest. Catholic priests actually did that? And then for Brando to tell him to go to Hell? Well, that was near blasphemy, but I was delighted by it just the same!

At those Saturday matinees before TV we also watched newsreels bringing us weekly news from around the world, as well as cartoons and serials, such as "Flash Gordon," starring Buster Crabbe, followed by films like *Tarzan of the Apes*, starring Johnny Weissmuller, the Olympic swimming champion.

I was also a member of the Roy Rogers Fan Club and looked forward to every Saturday when Roy would ride up to the camera on his horse, Trigger, and address the audience of kids. I even won a small statue of Trigger one Saturday, and kept in in my bedroom for years, although I don't remember what happened to it. Some of the kids in the audience, including me, felt we had a special relationship with Roy, since he was born in Cincinnati some thirty years earlier as Leonard Slye. I especially liked the song, "Tumblin' Tumbleweeds," which he sang with his musical group, Sons of the Pioneers.

Roy Rogers and Gene Autry were the prototypes of Hollywood's "Singing Cowboys" in the 1930s and '40s. While I enjoyed Gene Autry's movies and his song "Back in the Saddle Again," he was no match for Roy Rogers. Other cowboys I enjoyed on the big screen were Johnny Mack Brown, Lash LaRue, and Bob Steele, all who achieved only a small amount of recognition because they made westerns for minor film companies. Years later I was pleasantly surprised when I saw Bob Steele play the bad guy who murders Elisha Cook, Jr. in *The Big Sleep*.

The Wild One (1953), with Marlon Brando and Lee Marvin, pitted rebellious young motorcyclists against the inhabitants of a small town. When asked what he was rebelling against, Marlon Brando replied, "Whadya got?" Most of the kids in the audience, me included, stood up and cheered wildly!

Blackboard Jungle (1955), starring Glenn Ford and Sidney Poitier, was a film that examined the futility of a young teacher who was trying to teach high-school English to rebellious inner-city kids. It also had a rock & roll soundtrack featuring the song "Rock Around the Clock," performed by Bill Haley and the Comets. "Rock Around the Clock" was my introduction to rock & roll music, and nothing was the same after that. Within a year of that movie Elvis Presley exploded onto the scene.

John Lennon once said, "Before Elvis there was nothing." In a way he was right, but there were also many artists who laid the groundwork for Elvis, including Bill Haley and Chuck Berry, who fused black rhythm and blues and white hillbilly country music to create rock 'n roll. Then came Elvis, and the rest is history.

Rebel Without a Cause (1955), starring James Dean, was also a tale of youngsters rebelling against the society their parents had helped to create. This film became our streetwise Philosophy 101 course, as James Dean and his friends brooded over the purpose of life in what they saw as the hypocritical world of their parents and society.

All three of these films were anti-authoritarian and anti-establishment, and they had an influence on shaping my character as a young boy, since I identified with the young men played by Poitier, Brando and Dean, and absorbed their way of thinking about society. By the time I was fifteen I was sympathetic to these screen rebels, because I came to feel that America, and the world in general, for that matter, treated some people better than others and was consequently in need of change. On a larger scale, these movies from the '50s also helped pave the way for the counter-cultural rebellion in America during the 1960s.

*****

I saw my last movie at the West Hills around 1958. Five years later the theater had closed down and I was reviewing movies for the *Xavier News*, and in the evenings I also worked as an usher at the Guild Theater in Clifton. The Guild and the Esquire theaters were the only two arthouse theaters in Cincinnati at the time. They were called arthouses because they screened mostly independent and foreign films, which were often much more interesting and provocative, more "artsy" than Hollywood films.

According to many conservative critics at the time, these films were considered antithetical to American values and were often considered lewd and bordering on pornography. I reviewed Roman Polanski's 1962 break-out film, *Knife in the Water*, which was on the Catholic Church's Index of "Condemned" movies. As a result, some alumni called for my expulsion from Xavier. My Jesuit administrators, to their credit, ignored those calls, and I continued to write reviews.

The most impressive film I saw while working at the Guild was Federico Fellini's *8 1/2*, which remains one of my all-time favorite films. It was screened nightly for two weeks, and every evening I stood at the back of the Guild theater, enthralled by the film's black-and-white cinematography and dreamlike choreography. It was like a nightly seminar on filmmaking. Content-wise, the film was condemned by the Catholic Church for its themes of adultery, Existentialism, Communism and anti-Catholicism. These were, I must confess, some of the reasons I was attracted to the film.

By 1968 I would be making my first student films at Ohio State University. Later, from 1975 to 2010, I taught film history, film production, screenwriting and acting at Rowan University in New Jersey. I consider myself very fortunate that I was able to relive many of my early viewing experiences at the West Hills Theater by screening some of the same movies I saw in my youth to thousands of college students. *On the Waterfront*, for example, was an eye-opening experience for my students, who often found it hard to believe that "old black-and-white films" could be so good!

I was never told what I had to teach in my film history courses, and while I found it important to screen the "classic" films every film student should see, over the years a number of the films I showed were also some of my personal favorites, such as *Casablanca, Citizen Kane, Double Indemnity, Bicycle Thieves, On the Waterfront, 8½, Cabaret, Easy Rider, Stagecoach, North by Northwest, Wings of Desire, The Manchurian Candidate* and *The Lives of Others*.

13

DEATH BY ALGEBRA

There is no illusion greater than fear.

~ Lao Tzu

Friar Tuck was my high-school algebra teacher. Well, he wasn't Robin Hood's imaginary friar, but he's the one I would cast in the role if I ever made a Robin Hood movie. My algebra teacher's real name was Father Aldric, a pot-bellied Franciscan priest at Roger Bacon High School in 1956. When he erased the blackboard he would take the eraser and start at the top, while his bulging stomach would accidentally erase the bottom simultaneously.

Most days Father Aldric walked around the hallways with a smile—and with chalk dust caked on the front of his Franciscan habit. Now and then he would crack a cynical joke in class at our expense, and he loved to throw erasers at students he spotted dozing off in the back row. But most of the time he seemed rather serious and stern, especially when he was at the blackboard explaining to us the ins and outs of Algebra 1, all of which I couldn't comprehend then, and still don't understand today.

It was near the end of the semester when Father Aldric called me into his office for my semester review. He told me that I was flunking algebra, and that I should go home and tell my parents that I would probably have to go to summer school to get my grade high enough to pass the course. The news terrified me, not only because I didn't want to face summer school, but also because I didn't want to undergo the shame associated with being a failure. Both my older brothers had passed algebra with ease.

I left Father Aldric's office in a quandary. What could I do to avoid this embarrassment? Hide somewhere until it passed? Run away from home? After fretting over my options in the days that followed, I finally decided that I would go to my mother, tell her the dilemma I faced, and hope she would break the news to my father.

It was a warm and pleasant Saturday afternoon in early April just before Easter when I decided to walk to the poultry store on Queen City Avenue across the street from the Shadwell Park swimming pool. This was where my mother worked a couple of days a week to earn some extra cash for the family. I had never been to that store before, and I had some anxiety as I walked there, rehearsing what I would tell Mom about Father Aldric and algebra.

When I walked through the door Mom was standing next to the counter. She was wearing a large rubber apron that covered her from neck to knees, and rubber boots from the knees on down. For just a moment I wondered why she would be dressed that way, but the moment passed as I tried to concentrate on the speech I had concocted to tell her.

Pleasantly surprised by my appearance, she smiled and asked, "Richard! Why are you here?" while busily placing fresh cut chicken breasts on top of the ice in the display case. I opened my mouth to speak, but before I could respond she said, "Come here a minute. I want to show you something."

She quickly ushered me into an adjacent room that was empty, except for a line of large tin funnels bolted to one wall. The bottoms of the funnels were about two feet off the floor. The only other object in the room was a garden hose trickling out a stream of water that ran down a drain hole in the middle of the cement floor. I stood there wondering what the purpose of this vacant room was. When I turned to ask Mom, she was gone, but then she immediately reappeared, now wearing elbow-length rubber gloves and carrying two squawking live chickens by their legs, which she proceeded to stuff upside down into the funnels. Back and forth she went, fetching more and more chickens, until she had stuffed eight of them into the funnels.

I still had no idea what was happening, perhaps because I didn't want to know. But the chickens, jostling and squealing in their funnels, seemed to understand. Mom pulled all their heads out of the bottom of the funnels, then turned to me with a sly grin on her face as she picked up a small butcher knife from the counter.

"Watch," she said.

Starting at the first funnel, she bent down and sliced the neck of the first chicken, and then went down the line, quickly cutting the necks of all eight of the chickens. It was a ghastly sight, and I stood there wide-eyed with my mouth wide open, hardly believing what I was seeing, and not wanting to believe that my mother was capable of doing such a thing! The chickens were squawking and squirming in their death throes, and the red blood from their severed necks gushed out in unison, like a row of fountains—in this case, blood fountains.

Then suddenly one of the chickens escaped from its funnel and began running wildly around the room spewing blood. It was literally a chicken with his head cut off!

"Watch out, Mom!" I screamed.

"Don't worry," she said calmly in a voice of experience, "it'll fall over in a few seconds."

Which is exactly what it did. Mom then took all the dead chickens and tossed them into a large vat of boiling water which would render them easier to pluck and clean in a matter of minutes. The putrid smell of blood and dead chickens permeated the air, and I was close to vomiting. I realized then that I was standing in the middle of a killing room floor, and for a moment I feared that I might be the next victim of my mother's butcher knife, once I told her about summer school and algebra. I stood there, frozen in fright, while Mom began to hose down the blood splattered all over the funnels and walls of the room.

"Now, she asked, "what were you going to tell me?"

With a lump in my throat, I blurted out to her, "Father Aldric told me to tell you that I was flunking algebra and that I might have to go to summer school to repeat the class." I stood there awaiting my fate as I watched the blood swirl down the drain and smelled the awful stench of the boiling chickens in the vat.

"That's too bad," Mom said, "but it could be worse. We'll just have to work it out. Don't worry about it. I'll tell your father."

Moments later, as I left the gore and stench of the store and walked out into the fresh April air, I felt liberated, as if I had just been released from prison. I had confessed my shortcomings to my mother, and it seemed that summer school would be my only punishment. Mom was a saint!

At the end of the semester, fearing the worst, I opened my report card, only to discover that Father Aldric had given me a gift I didn't deserve: a passing grade of 70 (69 was flunking)! I'm happy to report that the summer of 1956 turned out to be a very pleasant one, but never again did I visit my mother at the poultry store. The fountains of blood still haunt me to this very day. So does algebra.

14

MY LIFE WITH WILLIAM SHAKESPEARE

*Life's but a walking shadow, a poor player
that struts and frets his hour upon the stage
and then is heard no more.*

Macbeth
~ William Shakespeare

My first encounter with William Shakespeare had profound impact on me. I was a sixteen-year-old junior at Roger Bacon High School in the Spring of 1958 when Mr. Hilvers, our English teacher, told us one Friday afternoon that we would begin reading Shakespeare's *Macbeth* in class on the following Monday, and that over the weekend our assignment was to read the first act of the play.

"You might not understand much of it," he said, "but read it anyway, and read the introduction to the play. We'll discuss it on Monday."

Like many high school students, I usually didn't crack a textbook on weekends, since weekends were reserved for my social life. But perhaps it was raining that Saturday night, or maybe I didn't have a date, so I opened my literature book and began to read Act I of *Macbeth*. Almost immediately something like a miracle occurred: the pages of the book appeared to become illuminated, and a whole new world revealed itself to me. I felt that rush of excitement one experiences when something new and full of wonder presents itself. Contrary to what Mr. Hilvers had said, I found that I understood the play from the very first lines onward, and as I read it I could see the action unfolding in my mind's eye.

I was immediately astonished by Shakespeare's words and how beautifully he put them together. I'd never experienced such writing before. I could almost feel the words, not through my senses, but through my heart, and they awakened me to a new reality from a slumber of ignorance. His words revealed images and ideas I had already been thinking about intuitively, even though I never realized I had been thinking them. It was as if these thoughts were simmering in the anteroom of my consciousness, just waiting to be revealed and validated by his words. This, I later realized, is what all true artists do. They reveal to us the secrets we already know and feel instinctively, even though we are unable to articulate them.

"Do you mean," I wondered to myself as I read, "that people are actually *allowed* to write this way?" Well, obviously they were, although I'd never encountered such writing before. Entranced, I read the whole play in the next two hours, and then I read the introduction.

On the following Monday the English class met again, and when Mr. Hilvers entered the classroom he asked, "Who can tell us what this play is about?" Immediately my hand shot up and he called on me. I stood up, and for the next five minutes or so I expounded on what I had learned over the weekend. I spoke about how Shakespeare wrote this play that takes place in Scotland, because James I, who had recently ascended to the English throne after the death of Queen Elizabeth I, was formerly

King James IV of Scotland, and that one of the characters in the play, Banquo, was believed to be James' ancestor and the founder of the Stuart line of Scottish kings to which James belonged. I also pointed out that Shakespeare was a member of the King's Men, a theater company subsidized by the king, and he wrote this play to honor King James.

Mr. Hilvers complimented me on my presentation, and I felt exhilarated by the experience. Behind me sat Jack Callopy, captain of the football team. When I sat down he poked me hard in the back with the eraser head of his pencil. Leaning forward, he jokingly whispered in my ear, "Grupenhoff, what the *hell* are you doing?" I smiled, and for a brief moment I considered what it must be like to be a teacher. Little did I realize then that in a few years I would be doing just that.

It was my first encounter with Shakespeare, and the only one for the time being. The next year I finished high school and, since I had no money to even consider going to college, I immediately joined the Navy. Three years later, in 1962, I returned home and entered college as an English major at Xavier University. In my sophomore year I wrangled my way into an upper-level Shakespeare class taught by Mr. Feldhaus, who told me it would be tough going.

"You'll be lucky to get a B in this class," he warned me. But I approached that class with much enthusiasm, and I particularly enjoyed taking roles and reading character's dialogue aloud as we read through the plays—which often reminded me of those early reading contests I was a part of in grade school. I did well enough in the class, and Mr. Feldhaus gave me (grudgingly, I think) a B in the course.

That experience led me in the following year, 1964, to try out for a play with the Masque Society, the campus theater group. The play was Shakespeare's *Measure for Measure*, and it was being staged to celebrate the 400th anniversary of his birth in 1564. I not only got a part, but it was the lead role, Duke Vincentio. My happiness with getting the role was soon tempered by the realization that I had to memorize all these lines of blank verse. As I began to learn the lines and go to rehearsals, I came to realize that acting was not as easy as it looked, and my fear of forgetting lines soon manifested itself in my dreams, where at times I not only didn't know my lines, but I had no idea what play I was in! Luckily, my dreams did not carry over into reality, and I played the role successfully—or, at least, as successfully as a first-time performer of Shakespeare could.

Program for "Measure for Measure," Xavier University, 1964.

Soon after I attended a professional production of Shakespeare's *The Merchant of Venice* at the Cincinnati Shakespeare Festival, which was then held at Our Lady of Cincinnati College. The show was not mounted on a proscenium arch stage; rather, it was set on the auditorium floor, surrounded on three sides by the audience. I was amazed by the creative staging and the openness it provided, along with the fact that the actors now passed within a few feet of me as they played their roles, and I could almost reach out and touch them. I felt I was part of the world of Venice unfolding before me. Clearly I was hooked on Shakespeare.

The following year I auditioned and was cast as Benvolio in that same company's production of Shakespeare's *Romeo and Juliet*, and it was there that I really began to learn what Shakespeare was all about. We staged about 20 productions of the play over a three-week period.

One evening, about 15 performances into the production, I entered the stage on my cue in Act I, and I stepped into what seemed to me to be an entirely new production of the play. The same lines we had spoken in earlier performances were now being delivered differently. That is, specific words were being delivered with a different emphasis than before, which, in turn, almost intuitively caused the next actor to deliver his lines with different stresses or nuances to them. I knew my lines, but I too delivered them in a different way without even thinking I was doing so.

I felt I was in an entirely new play, even though it was the same one we had been performing for the past two weeks. The audience was seeing *Romeo and Juliet* with the same lines, of course, but it was not the same play we had performed the night before. This was a revelation that I will never forget, and I realized that one of the main differences between a live theater performance and a film is that the live performance is different every night, while film is a one-time performance frozen on celluloid. But more importantly, I came to understand that Shakespeare's words contained layers of meaning and subtle nuances that permitted them to be interpreted and delivered in different ways. That richness of language is one of the elements that makes his plays universal, so that even today, over four hundred years later, the plays still move us.

A few months after that production I married Carolyn O'Donnell, and within a year I had graduated from Xavier and we had our first-born child, Richard Dylan, who was born in Cincinnati on August 1, 1966, and the following month we went off to graduate school at Purdue University. Our second son, James Cullen, was born while we were there on February 24, 1968. In August of that year I received my Master of Arts degree in American Studies. Although I had enjoyed my stay there, I was itching to get back into theater. I applied for and won a fellowship to Ohio State University in the Theater Department's Ph.D. program. During my years there I wrote and directed three plays and acted in many more.

In the summer of 1976 I was doing professional work again, this time at the Alabama Shakespeare Festival, where I had roles in Shakespeare's *The Winter's Tale, King Lear* and *The Merry Wives of Windsor*, and in Moliere's *The Miser*. My role of Gloucester in *King Lear* was, by my own estimation, the best role I ever played, and that production of *King Lear* was the highlight of my acting career.

A year earlier, in 1975, I had taken a job teaching film production and film history at Glassboro State College in New Jersey (later, in 1992, it became Rowan University). As the years passed I became more and more involved in scholarship, teaching, and raising a family. I took part in fewer theater productions, although I did perform in some student productions, such as *The Tempest*, in which I played Prospero. I also appeared in *Romeo and Juliet* twice, both times playing the Prince, once in 1977, and again, more than thirty years later, in 2011. I turned 70 that year, and that was my last formal stage appearance.

In 1994 I traveled to London with my partner, Carol Ann, and we visited Shakespeare's birthplace in Stratford-on-Avon. It was a spiritual and artistic homecoming for me, and I found myself trembling with excitement as I walked through the house where he is said to have been born. On that same trip we visited the construction of the replica of Shakespeare's Globe Theatre in London and vowed to return when the theater was completed.

It took us twenty years, but in 2014 we went back to London and saw *Julius Caesar* and *Antony and Cleopatra* at the new Globe. Tears welled up in my eyes when I entered the theater, and I felt that I was home again. By this time every theater was like a church to me, a sacred, ritual space where the human condition could be explored and celebrated. It was always my dream to act in one of Shakespeare's plays on the Globe's stage, if only as a spear-carrier or another extra, non-speaking role, but at this point of my life I'm afraid that is one wish on my bucket list that will go unfulfilled.

In 2014 I came out of retirement to teach a course in Shakespeare for the English Department at Rowan University. Teaching Shakespeare at the university level was the crowning glory of my relationship with Shakespeare, an involvement that had begun in that high-school English class with Mr. Hilvers in 1958. I never imagined then that fifty-six years later I would be teaching Shakespeare to university students.

In the summer of 2016, Carol Ann and I visited Sicily. One of the sights we saw there was the open-air Greek theater in Segesta, located atop Mount Barbaro, complete with a sweeping view of the valley below and the Mediterranean Sea beyond. Here is where the plays of Sophocles, Aeschylus and Euripides were performed by Greek actors as early as 300 BC.

As an actor I couldn't resist the opportunity to perform on the same stage that actors have been performing on for over 2,000 years. I immediately walked on stage and performed Gloucester's "We have seen the best of our times" soliloquy from *King Lear*, in front of about 20 tourists, who applauded my two-minute performance. Since 2016 marked the 400th anniversary of Shakespeare's death, I had encompassed Shakespeare's life cycle of 52 years—from my first production of *Measure for Measure* in 1964 that celebrated the 400th anniversary of his birth, to my brief two-minute monologue in the Greek theatre of Segesta, 52 years later.

Today I sit in my study and read Shakespeare's plays and frequently discover new ideas and images in his work. I continue to marvel—just as I did when I first read *Macbeth* in high school over sixty years ago—at Shakespeare's creative use of language and his brilliant sense of theatrical staging. My life has been blessed and enriched by knowing this man through his plays and poetry. More than once I have been asked the question, "If you had a chance to sit down and speak with anyone who ever lived, who would it be?" My answer is always, "Will Shakespeare."

DEAR WILL

>Even now, after all these centuries,
>there are those who still find ways to doubt you,
>doubt that the son of a mere Stratford glover
>who did not attend university
>could compose such beautiful poetry.
>Marlowe (also a glover's son), who went
>to lofty Cambridge, these skeptics embrace.
>
>Yet, these elitists, today's Robert Greenes,
>university wits all, who dub you
>an upstart crow, cannot explain your gift,
>but yet they denigrate you, not knowing
>that your "little Latin and less Greek"
>was far more than they'll ever know, and your

memorization of Plautus, Ovid
and Seneca is the classical soil
from which your poetry and drama spring.

And none of them, I'll wager, rarely trod
the boards, and if they did they might have been
that "poor player who struts and frets his hour
upon the stage and then is heard no more."

They fail to see that your work at The Globe
as an actor, playwright and producer
made all your wonderful plays bring to life
those characters who still live among us.
And no contemporary, no deVere,
could ever make such an essential claim.

And so, until they find the evidence
that all these words do not belong to you,
I'll always believe, without hesitance,
it was your pen from which such beauty grew.

15

MARY WHITE

Everything has beauty,
but not everyone sees it.

~ Confucius

By all normal standards of physical beauty, Mary White was not. No doubt about it. One side of her jaw was mangled, making that side of her mouth droop down, so much so that now and then her lip got caught between her teeth, causing her speech to be slightly slurred. No one knew how her mouth became so disfigured, and none of us asked. Some guessed it was the act of a maniacal dentist who had damaged her jaw when she was a child, while others speculated she had some sort of disease or cancer that required part of her jawbone to be removed.

Mary White was the soda jerk at our teen-age hangout during my high school years, "Queen Anne's Confectionary," a rather pretentious name for a tiny, one-room soda shop in South Fairmount on the west side of Cincinnati in the mid-1950s. Mary, who was about 40 years old at the time, was not only our dispenser of Cherry Cokes, banana splits and root-beer floats, she was also our confidant and sometime surrogate mother, providing advice for those of us who sought it. We were the children she never had.

Mary watched me and my friends grow from wet-behind-the-ears teenagers to fairly mature (or so we thought) high-school seniors. Some of us had revealed to her a few secrets from our lives, for we were able to talk openly with her about our dreams and desires. I had conversations with her that I wouldn't dare have with my parents, or even my friends. Sometimes, when no one else was in the shop, I would sit alone at the counter sipping my cherry Coke and telling her my problems. It was sort of like going to confession to a priest, only much better, because Mary would always be supportive and, instead of giving me penance, she would top off my cherry Coke free of charge.

It was during these high school days that I became attracted to a little redhead girl from North Fairmount who would often meet me at Queen Anne's in the early evenings, and I would walk her back home after sunset. Mary had intuited the depth of our romance, and she warned me to be careful, reminding me that the consequences could be ruinous. She kept an eye on us, telling us not to act out displays of affection in front of other customers as we sat at our table dreamy-eyed, sipping our sodas while singing along to the Platters' "Only You," playing on the juke box next to the candy case.

Never once in four years did my buddies that I hung out with in Queen Anne's have a bad word for Mary, despite the fact that we were brash and crude teenage boys, and never once do I recall any of us make fun of her disfigurement, even when she wasn't around. I suppose it was because we all valued her impact upon our lives. We were incapable of articulating it at the time and, in fact, I don't think we were very conscious of it, but I believe we all loved her for who she was.

My life at Queen Anne's came to an end in 1959 when I graduated from high school and joined the Navy and sailed half-way around the world. When I returned home three years later in 1962 the neighborhood had begun to change. Queen Anne's was out of business, and Mary was gone from my life—or so I thought.

Then one day, about thirty years later, while on a return visit to Cincinnati, I somehow discovered that Mary was in an assisted-living home, and before I left town I decided to visit her. By this time, she was bedridden, living with about eight other elderly women in a dormitory setting. Although I could tell she was embarrassed to have me visit her in this place while she was in such poor physical condition, she was happy to see me and asked about my life and what I was up to. We began to trade stories, picking up where we left off thirty years ago. No, I told her, I didn't marry the little redhead from North Fairmount, and yes, I'd lost touch with my buddies I had hung out with years ago in Queen Anne's, and now I was a professor at a university in New Jersey, married with two sons in college.

We traded stories for about an hour, but by then it became apparent that we were running out of things to say, and I realized she was growing physically tired from so much talk. So, after a few moments of silence, we said our goodbyes. When I got to the door I turned to her and smiled, and she smiled back. But they were bittersweet smiles, for while we were happy to have reconnected, we both knew this was the last time we would see each other in this lifetime, and that this was the end of our relationship that began many years before at Queen Anne's.

As I closed the door behind me and stepped outside into the warm sunlight, I stopped for a moment and thought that, despite her physical deformity, Mary was one of the most beautiful women I had ever known.

*Queen Anne's Confectionary, Christmas Eve, 1957.
Back row from left: Me, Frank (?), "Boomer" (?), Alan Hammann.
Front: Steve Weber, Jerry Luensman. Photo by Mary White.*

16

JOSEPH HENDKER

Never forget that you are one of a kind.

~ R. Buckminster Fuller

I began working at Brighton Furniture in the summer of 1956, just after my freshman year in high school. It was a job I inherited from my brother, John, who had recently graduate from college. My daily duties were to dust the kitchen and bedroom furniture, sweep off the living room couches, and mop the floors. Once a week I washed and squeegeed the front display windows.

My boss was Joseph Hendker, the owner of the store. He had been born in Glandorf, Germany (only a few miles south of Osnabrück) in 1904, and he came in America in 1928 "with only fifty cents in my pocket," as he used to say. Yet, within twenty years he had worked his way up from carpentry and constructing coffins to owning his own store, Brighton Furniture—and making a very good living at it, too.

One's life is shaped by the people one meets and interacts with, and Mr. Hendker was one of those who played a significant role in mine.

He taught me many practical things, like how to judge the quality of different fabrics, and how good craftsmanship could be rated by analyzing how well a dresser drawer was constructed. But he also taught me the necessity of treating people with respect and concern for their well-being.

He had numerous customers who had bought furniture from him on credit with only a down payment, and he often let them slide when they came in and told him they couldn't make the payment that month. He would put his arm around their shoulder and commiserate with them and tell them to come back when they got the money. Never once in three years did I witness any of them failing to return, and never did he have to repossess any of the furniture he had sold.

During my time working for him Mr. Hendker became something of a father figure for me. On slow days when there were no customers, he would have me sit down with him and we would have long discussions about life and the world and the news of the day as he blew smoke rings from his ever-present cigar. His thoughts and opinions were not always positive, however. He had his prejudices. Now and then he would express his dislike of certain people, and I would try to counter his arguments with my own growing sense of social equality and justice. Despite his prejudices, at his core he was a good man, and when I left for the Navy he gave me a warm bear hug, a tearful goodbye and some very good advice—all things my father never gave me.

One of the most important ideas Mr. Hendker taught me was that there was no such thing as a sale, because when a store says it is having a sale it is merely cutting back on the profit they would make on the product. One rarely, if ever, buys a product at a retail store at less than the wholesale cost of the item to the store owner. The idea of a sale was to move merchandise that was going out of season or was otherwise difficult to move.

A sale, he taught me, is often based on deception. He gave me an example: "See this lamp in the window? It's been here a long time, and I want to get rid of it. The price has been $25, so I will make a new sign: SALE – was $40, now $25. That should do it," he said, placing the new sign in front of the lamp. Sure enough, the lamp was sold within a week.

I worked year-round in the store for almost three years, logging in about 12 hours a week for $15, which wasn't too bad in the 1950s – a little over a dollar an hour! During the school year I would get out of class at Roger Bacon about 2:40 in the afternoon and take the bus to Brighton. I arrived at the store around 3:30, and worked until 5:30, mopping the floors, dusting the bedroom sets, and helping to uncrate new furniture that had recently been delivered. At 5:30 we would lock up the store and Mr. Hendker would drive me back across the Western Hills Viaduct in his 1957 Buick Road Master Riviera and drop me off by the Spring Garden Bank at the intersection of Harrison and Westwood Avenues, and then he would head home to Cheviot.

He told me that when he bought the car he went to the Buick dealer's showroom dressed in his shabby old gardening clothes. The reason he did this was to find out how willing the salesman was to consider him a viable customer.

"The first salesman didn't want to have anything to do with me," he said. "But the second one was very nice, and he stayed with me and closed the deal. Imagine the first salesman's surprise when he saw me pay the full price of the car with a check, right then and there!"

It was a good lesson for me, but I was equally impressed that he was able to pay the full price for the car right away, about $3,500. I admired him for that. Nobody I knew had that kind of money in their savings account. In fact, my parents never even had a savings account; we lived from paycheck to paycheck. Over fifty years later, when I bought a new car and paid the full price in cash, I thought warmly of Mr. Hendker, and I knew he would have approved.

After I left for the Navy I continued to correspond with him, sending him brief notes about where I was and what sites I was seeing, along with monthly amounts of cash that he would take to the Provident Bank at Brighton Corner and deposit in the savings account I had set up for college. When I returned from the Navy three years later I took my old job back for a few weeks, but I couldn't stay there long because I realized I wasn't making enough money and had to find a better job. I promised to stop by now and then to visit with him, which I did, but my visits soon tapered off.

The last time I saw him was in the summer of 1965, when I dropped by to tell him I was getting married, and he gave me a new box spring and mattress as a wedding present. Then, just two years later in the spring of 1967, while I was in graduate school at Purdue University, I stumbled across his obituary in the Cincinnati paper, and I was stunned. He was only 64 when he died, and it saddens me to this day that I never had a chance to say goodbye to him and to thank him for all he had done for me. He was one of a kind.

17

LIFE LESSONS

Face your life, its pain and its pleasure.

The Graveyard Book
~ Neil Gaiman

When I was growing up my family members were fairly tolerant of each other, and we hardly ever expressed hurtful words that turned into angry arguments; rather, we learned to avoid confrontations by repressing our feelings. There was very little physical punishment, aside from the occasional spanking that was common in those days to keep the kids in line. Emotions were blanketed over, however, and displays of love, anger, joy and sorrow were rarely expressed. In short, our house was emotionally colorless, no highs or lows, just a constant dull greyness.

Love was not a part of our family's daily interaction. None of us ever expressed care or concern for one another upon meeting, and no one ever said, "I love you," upon departure (although that phrase was not as commonly used then as it is today). Never once did I see my mother and father embrace in the privacy of our house, never saw them kiss or display affection in those tender moments when you might expect it to happen. The only times they embraced in front of their children was when they were dancing. Happily, they were very good dancers, and it was a pleasure to watch them.

To friends and neighbors, we probably appeared to be a rather well-balanced family. The truth is, however, that we were an emotionally stunted and dysfunctional family, each of us self-censoring, unable to articulate our basic needs and desires to the other. We lived our lives in a kind of emotional paralysis.

Like most kids, I had many days filled with physical pain from minor accidents like scraped knees, and sicknesses like measles, mumps and whooping cough. But even worse than the physical pain I underwent was the emotional pain I suffered, that daily pain of feeling abandoned, ostracized, ignorant and unimportant. There was also the pain of being told I wasn't good enough, that I was inferior. Moreover, I was also a sinner in the eyes of God, and the nuns filled me with guilt because they said that my sins were the nails that hung Christ upon the cross. I came to believe I was destined to go to Hell when I died if I didn't do what I was told. My ego wasn't strong enough to resist and deny all these daily charges against me, so I believed them all. I came to feel that I would never measure up, and it was all my fault. I was, in my own mind, guilty as charged.

Recent scientific studies of brain scans reveal that such emotional rejection is actually experienced as physical pain, whether that rejection is caused by family, friends or strangers. Because I wanted to avoid such emotional pain I became fearful of expressing my wishes and desires, and fearful of meeting new people or going to new places. I pretty much kept to myself. The constant emotional rejection and lack of love made me timid and bashful. There I was, feeling unloved and unrecognized, even by my own family. As the fourth of six children I felt ignored, and whatever goals I achieved went unnoticed and unrewarded.

Nor do I recall anyone giving me a positive boost to my ego. In my mind, my older brothers received all the academic and sports accolades, my younger sisters all the attention and caring. It's a wonder that I was able to overcome my lack of self-esteem and confidence and lead a rather successful life. If my parents were alive today they probably would deny that the ignored me, or that they loved me less than their other children.

Still, to be clear and honest about it, there were days when I felt happy, and our family life was enjoyable. I remember, for example, how happy I was the day my older brother Paul returned from Korea, for when he left to join the Army I thought I might never see him again. The first day he came back I asked him to sit with me in front of the TV and watch Fess Parker play Davy Crockett, "King of the Wild Frontier." While we were watching, I showed him the Davy Crockett coonskin hat Mom had bought me. It was an early advertising gimmick that for a few weeks was all the rage. Paul thought the hat was funny-looking, and I can still hear his laughter. But when I asked him if he wanted to try it on, he only grinned and pushed it back down on my head.

Just over fifty years later, in 2006, Paul died at his home in Michigan. After the funeral I was driving to the airport with Carol Ann and my brother John. We stopped at a convenience store and Carol Ann ran in to pick up a few things for us to munch on as we headed to the airport. John and I waited in the car, sitting in silence for a few moments. Then John turned to me and said, "Richard, I don't feel anything about Paul." It seemed as if he wanted to grieve our brother's passing, but he couldn't because he didn't know how to do it.

"What do you expect?" I said. "We grew up in a family that was unable to express our feelings, and we never learned to love and depend on one another." My response surprised him, and it even surprised me, because I had never really thought about our family life in that way before. But it was true. Our parents never taught us how to love, perhaps because they were never taught how by their own parents. They never taught us, at least by example, how to express our emotions (or that we were allowed to). So, sitting in this car in a convenience store parking lot on a dreary day in Detroit, my brother and I were unable to grieve the loss of our eldest brother.

Over the years I came to resent my parents for this, but as I grew older I realized that the best thing for me to do was to accept them for who they were, and to appreciate all the good things they did for us, especially when I considered that they had six children and very little money in those days. It was only through this acceptance that I freed myself from those unhappy feelings of my past, which then finally allowed me to feel and express love for my parents. Unfortunately, I came to this realization only after they had both passed away, so I never had a chance to express those loving feelings to them personally. Without a guide, I had to teach myself how to love them. I had to teach myself how to love, period. One of my life-long regrets is that I think I didn't always do a very good job of giving and receiving love. Even today I could be better at it, especially with those close to me.

I came to understand that I had been emotionally damaged when I was very young and, as a result, my confidence, my sense of self, and my imagination were stunted and inhibited by the common behavioral requirements of the various social groups in my life: my family, church, school, and the world at large. From the moment we are born we are inundated and indoctrinated with certain cultural cues and biases that reflect the philosophies and prejudices of the society at large, and It took me a long time to realize that society's common goal was to "normalize" me, so that I would be accepted into society, to "fit in."

One by-product of such social engineering is often the erasure of desire and imagination, so whatever creative instincts I might have had at the time were almost always repressed. By annihilating desire, my will to choose was erased, and since I had no desire, no passion, I had no principle of action, and no motive to act. I drifted through the days of my childhood with few thoughts and fewer emotions, flying through space and time like a zombie pilot, attending only to my senses and their needs. As a result, I had no goals, no dreams for the future. I developed no real personality in those days, and I had a limited sense of identity. I operated mostly on suggestion, and I only wanted to please everyone, hoping that would make my life better, too. I came to believe that I was born to please and serve others. Pleasing myself was not an option; it was out of the question.

I grew up willing to do what others wanted me to do. I didn't want to disappoint them or hurt their feelings. I was servile to almost everyone I knew: to my parents, to nuns and priests, even to strangers I would meet, and to anyone who wanted or allowed me to please them. If and when they responded positively to my attention, I felt accepted, and at times I unwittingly translated those feelings into what I thought was love, but it was not that at all. Rather, it was me fulfilling some inner, psychological need for attention and recognition that masqueraded as love. But this "love" was all pretense, devoid of any emotional attachment, no feelings of happiness or fulfillment on my part, no feelings that my life was validated or authentic, and no positive feelings of love for the other.

I'm reminded of the movie, *Zelig*, Woody Allen's pseudo-documentary film in which he played the title role. After watching that film, I realized that in a very real way I was just like Zelig when I was younger. Here was a man so void of emotions, so unfeeling that he could adjust to any social situation, not by expressing who he was, but by sublimating his ego (what there was of it), and by operating mostly on suggestions made by others.

Unaware of who he was, Zelig became the person those around him wanted him to be. He had buried his emotions, and without any emotional reaction the only thing that saved Zelig was his intellect. If there were a situation that needed solving, he could do it. Yet his life was determined by people and events over which he had no control. He wanted to please others, not himself. He wanted them to define his life, to tell him what to do, to tell him who to be. That's exactly how I felt when I was young.

Woody Allen once ruefully remarked, "My only regret in life is that I am not someone else." I often felt I wanted to be someone else, too, and perhaps that's why I became involved in theater and film later in my life. As an actor I could, at least for an hour or two on stage, be someone else, and as a writer and director I could create worlds opposed to the gray, lonely world of my childhood. Theater, film, and art in general became therapeutic exercises for my psychic health. Art made me feel things, not just experience them. And it made me feel good.

Luckily, as the years passed, I was able to overcome my Zelig impulses and develop a greater sense of who I was. As a result of my life experiences, I developed an inner resistance to "fitting in," and found an unconscious need to protect and nourish my creative imagination, to seek something else that was out there for me, even though I didn't realize that that was what I was doing.

My early alienation from most things social rendered me an observer of life, rather than a full participant. It was a stance that was to have both positive and negative consequences. By watching others I could analyze their behavior and deduce some psychological generalities about why people do the things they do. On the other hand, I never felt part of the unfolding social events and experiences around me, although I did try to conform and be part of things, but usually to no avail. When I was young I was an observer of life, rarely an active participant.

By the time I was eight years old I dimly began to feel that I was different from most kids my age, who appeared to me to be much happier and more well-balanced socially. They seemed to get along better in the world of adults and adult values than I did. They were more outgoing, while I was shy and retiring. But I also began to feel that many of the adults around me considered me different from the other kids my age. I don't know why they would have thought that. I would like to think that they saw something special in me, but I doubt they did, and I certainly saw nothing special in me. I felt that I was different in a negative sense, never a positive one.

All this led to my lack of self-confidence and self-esteem, which then led to my inability to set life goals because, after all, I came to believe that I was such a failure and such a sinner that I didn't deserve success, and past experiences had convinced me I was doomed to defeat in whatever undertaking I considered. So, throughout my formative years I was led not by reason, but by these painful emotions I was constantly trying to avoid. Withdraw and avoid pain. That was my strategy. Don't plan for tomorrow, just struggle to make it through today and the next day. And the next. Survival was the key.

Life became for me a waiting, a waiting for whatever would happen next. Sometimes I felt as if I were on a raft floating down the River of Time, without an oar, without a sail or rudder, just flowing with the current, allowing myself to be taken for a ride around the next bend, heading towards the next event over which I had little control. Circumstances and chance controlled my life. Obviously, I conducted very little self-reflection while I was growing up. Not once by the time I was 17 did I ever consider what my future goals would be.

"What are you planning to do after high school?" my girlfriend's father asked me one night during my senior year. No one had ever asked me that question, not even my parents.

"I don't know," I replied meekly.

"Okay," he said, and promptly rose from his chair and left the room. Just a day or two after that encounter my girlfriend ended our relationship. She never told me why, but it was obvious that her father didn't think I was good enough for her since I had no plans for the future and hadn't even thought about going to college. Not once had I thought about or made plans to go to college. Not once had my parents sat me down and asked me what I wanted to do after I graduated from high school. And so I took whatever came along.

Then one day, about a month before I graduated, I had a conversation with a friend, Charlie Milazzo, who had recently been discharged from the Navy. He suggested that if I had no other options, I should think about joining the Navy. Without considering the consequences, that's exactly what I did. When I went to join up, the recruiting officer asked why I wanted to join the Navy. I responded stereotypically that I wanted to see the world, but I now realize that what I really wanted to do was to escape my dull, colorless home life and find out who I was—or, better yet, to discover who that person was that I was in the process of creating.

18

THREE YEARS BEFORE THE MAST

*The only person you are destined to
become is the person you decide to be.*

~ R.W. Emerson

In June 1959 I graduated from Roger Bacon High School, and my previous life came to an end. Now I had to make some decisions about my future. My high school advisor, Father Stanley, told me a few months before I graduated that he didn't think I was college material, and he suggested I should begin looking for a full-time job, perhaps in a factory somewhere. I felt inferior to my classmates who were moving on to college, but I had no money to go to college anyway. On the other hand, I had no desire to work in a factory for the rest of my life, either.

So, I bundled up my insecurities along with my toothbrush and razor and made the first big decision of my life when I joined the Navy on June 29, 1959. Just 17, I left home and was on my own for the first time. All I felt was that I wanted out of the world I was living in, hoping for something better. This is how the first real journey of my life began. I had cut the ropes binding me to my childhood past, sending me free-falling into the future, and I had no idea what was going to happen next.

I flew from Cincinnati to Chicago that night with a few other recruits. It was the first time I had flown in an airplane, a Delta prop plane seating about 50 passengers. The flight attendants passed out complimentary drinks and cigarettes for all, and by the time we were flying through the clouds, the interior of the plane had a cloud of its own, reeking with that bitter, greasy smell of alcohol and cigarette smoke.

We landed in Chicago around 9 p.m. and were transported by bus from the airport to the Navy's Great Lakes Training Center. Joining me on the bus were recruits from Philadelphia, Pittsburgh and Cincinnati, all of us away from home for the first time, trying to act mature by telling dirty jokes and boasting about girlfriends and neighborhoods left behind. I sat quietly in my seat, listening to their jabbering, smiling now and then at an off-colored joke, but mostly wondering whether I should even be there at all. I was feeling very anxious as the bus headed north and swallowed us up into the blackness of the night.

We arrived at the training camp about midnight and were immediately taken to an auditorium where we began to be processed out of civilian life. There were numerous forms to be filled out and signed, and we were given our military serial number, which would be our official identification until our discharge. My number was 479-88-01. We were then instructed to take the indelible pencil we found in our packets, rub spit on our left forearm, and write our number there in purple so that we would memorize it and constantly be reminded of who we were during the following weeks. So, I no longer had a name; now I was only a number.

I remember thinking about the stories I had read of the Jews who had been imprisoned in the Nazi concentration camps just fifteen years earlier, and I felt something of what they must have felt when their numbers were permanently tattooed into their flesh. While my future was not nearly as bleak as theirs, I nevertheless began to feel something of what it was like to undergo such a dehumanizing process. I began losing my sense of self and self-worth (what little I had of it), and I experienced feelings of helplessness as I transitioned into this authoritarian society I had chosen to join. Regular life was stifling enough, I thought, but this was much worse.

Civilian life and our civilian identities began to be stripped from us, and we were reprogrammed into military life, where we had little or no freedom to do what we pleased, and we were required to do what we were told to do or face a harsh punishment for disobeying. I found it interesting that some of the new recruits adapted to this regimen quite easily. Perhaps it was because they found meaning in having someone else make decisions for them, or perhaps it gave them a greater sense of self-worth, I don't know. What I do know is that from the very beginning I was involved in a program that was to take away some of the freedoms I had enjoyed as a civilian. But that's what the military demanded.

That first night we finally got to bed about 3 a.m. I was assigned an upper bunk, only about 18 inches or so beneath a steam pipe above me. Before I fell asleep I began to doubt that I had made the right decision by joining up, and I'm sure many of the others that night were thinking the same. Then and there I felt I had made a terrible mistake. So, to put my dilemma into perspective, I began to calculate the days until my 21st birthday, when I would be discharged—over a thousand days later! Could I last that long?

While considering my future that night, I made another important decision. Before I fell asleep I swore to myself that when I got out of the Navy my goal was to go to college. Where and how I was going to make that happen, I didn't know. All I know is that I was determined to do that. It was that dream, that goal, that helped me survive the next three years. That decision also helped me fall asleep.

Just three hours later, at 6 a.m., we were awakened by a horrible sound that seemed like machine-gun fire. I bolted up quickly, slamming my head into the steam pipe above me, and I fell back onto my pillow, seeing stars. Then I heard that noise again, this time accompanied by a voice that rang out, "Alright, you goddamn swabbies, hit the deck! You're in the Navy now!"

Hardly awake and with my head still spinning, I climbed down from my bunk and stood at attention. The voice belonged to a young officer who, I later discovered, had graduated from college just two or three weeks earlier, where he'd been a member of the Navy's Reserved Officer Training Corps. He was a newly minted ensign, and he had an empty Coke bottle in his hand that he swirled around the inside of a corrugated metal trash can over and over again, and the awful noise made my headache worse. The ensign was only about four years older than me, and I resented him from the moment I saw him.

It was grey and raining that morning as we washed up and shaved, even though many of us, including me, were still too young to actually grow whiskers. We were all stacked up on each other, about sixty young men trying to wedge our way to six water basins and toilets, while at the same time being prodded by the ensign in charge to hurry up, so we could march off to breakfast and begin our first full day of boot camp. After a stroke or two of my razor I gave up on shaving with cold water and went back to my bunk and got dressed.

After a miserable breakfast of cold scrambled eggs, greasy bacon, soggy toast and lukewarm coffee, we were herded into the barber shop, where bored civilian barbers shaved off our hair. We walked out of there almost bald, and some of us were visibly upset that this had been done to us. Once again I thought of the Nazi concentration camps and, although I knew our shorn hair was not going to be collected and used for other purposes, I still realized that this ritual of shaving my head was the Navy's way of erasing another part of my former identity.

Then we were marched to the drill hall, where we were stripped of our civilian clothes and given our uniforms, dungarees, underwear, shoes, hats and shirts, stenciling all of them with our name and serial number to avoid theft. We stuffed these clothes into our new duffel bags, which were to function as our luggage throughout our time in the Navy. So, within a matter of twenty-four hours I had developed a new identity. My hair, my clothes and my very will had been taken from me. I was now a seaman recruit in the United States Navy.

The ensuing eight weeks in boot camp was perhaps the unhappiest period of my life. Almost nightly I fell asleep disappointed with myself for enlisting, and angry about what I had been forced to do every day. Yet, perhaps because I was young, I was able to make it through those days. Some guys didn't, however, and at times we would return to our barracks in the afternoon only to find that one or two men were no longer with us, and that they had been shipped home on a general or medical discharge, either because they were psychologically unwilling or physically unable to continue.

One recruit, Glenn, was so depressed that he decided to urinate in his bunk every night. Those who slept near him grew angry because of the stench, and they bullied him and threatened him with bodily harm unless he shaped up or shipped out. After a visit to the base psychologist, he did indeed ship out—all the way home! He had been given a medical discharge.

I had been friends with Glenn since the day we joined up in Cincinnati. We had sat together and had gotten to know each other on the plane to Chicago. As he was packing up to leave he told me he just couldn't take it anymore. He had joined the Navy only because his father wanted him to, and now he was headed back home and was going to start college in September at the University of Cincinnati. Although I envied him for having the courage to do what he did, I chose to stick with it and hope that things would soon get easier.

They didn't. Reveille was at 6 a.m., and every morning after breakfast we went to the drill grounds for an hour or so to learn how to march in unison. That was followed by classes in seamanship, knot-tying, rifle shooting, and swimming. Then it was back to the barracks for inspection of our living spaces, conducted by training officers who fostered fear among us by constantly belittling us, constantly yelling at us, constantly finding fault with us. They called it "discipline."

Boot Camp, July 1959.

I don't remember smiling once during those eight weeks, except for the time I had my official boot camp photograph taken, and that smile was forced. I had no one to pour my soul out to. Sure, I wrote letters to my parents and friends, but I never burdened them by telling them how unhappy I was. Dad had sent me a subscription to the *Cincinnati Post*, so I was able to read the daily papers and use them as a kind of lifeline to the non-military world I had left behind.

One of my most depressing moments in boot camp came when I received a letter from my older brother, John, who scolded me for joining the Navy, and he told me how disappointed he was to hear of it. He said that he could have gotten me into the University of Texas, where he was presently enrolled in graduate school. All I had to do was ask him. That really upset me. Why didn't he make that offer weeks ago before I graduated from high school? I would have gladly gone. Now I simply felt abandoned by him as well, and I didn't answer his letter.

After the first two weeks things began to settle down as the routine became familiar and my depression began to lift. I began to understand how the system worked, and how to work the system to avoid the worst parts of boot camp. And I did just that. For example, one day a request came for volunteers from our company to serve in the "Color Guard," a four-man detail that carried flags and rifles at the beginning of parades and at weekly graduations. I jumped at the opportunity, for I had heard that their practice was to take place inside a hall at the same time as those mind-numbing marching exercises my company had to endure on the drill grounds in the sweltering July sun.

I was assigned to one group of four and, along with about ten other groups from different companies, we began to learn how to march with the flags, or "colors." We learned how to march together, how to turn and change directions and look quite smart and proud doing it. After a while, my team was given a break, and we sat and watched the other groups do their drills. We came to realize that some of these teams were better than we were, and that they would be the ones chosen to be the standard bearers for the graduations that occurred every weekend.

When we went outside for a cigarette break the idea came to us: let's deliberately be mediocre in our drills, not bad enough to be kicked out and returned to our company, but only just not good enough to be chosen to lead the parade at the next graduation. This would save us from having to drill with the rest of our company outside in the sweltering sun, and it would also free us up for the weekends, on one of which we were going to receive a twelve-hour pass to spend in Chicago or Milwaukee. No need to jeopardize that!

For the next four weeks or so we went daily to our practice, performing well enough to be allowed to remain, but lack-luster enough not to be chosen for the next parade. While our company mates drilled outside in the August heat, we drilled inside the much cooler hall, taking breaks now and then to go outside and sit in the shade and smoke cigarettes and eat Baby Ruth candy bars we had purchased at the canteen, while telling each other stories about girls we had known back home. Although I can't say life then was good, at least we had found a way to make it more tolerable.

Boot camp lasted about eight weeks, and somewhere in the middle I had an interview to determine where I would be stationed after basic training was over. I turned down radio school because it would have required me to stay an extra year in the Navy, and I turned down yeoman's school because I didn't want to be a secretary in an office on some Naval air base. When asked, I told them that what I wanted was to go to sea, so they assigned me to Quartermaster School in Newport, Rhode Island. A quartermaster in the Navy had nothing to do with supplies, like in the Army. A Navy quartermaster had a number of duties, including navigation and signaling. I was pleased with that assignment, and things were looking up—or so I thought.

We received our first duty assignments in the final week of boot camp. When the list was posted I discovered I was assigned to the deck force of the U.S.S. Severn (AO-61), an inglorious World War II oil tanker homeported in Newport, Rhode Island. All this time I had assumed I was going to Quartermaster School, and while most of the other guys around me celebrated their school assignments, I sat down in my bunk, disappointed once again. Par for the course, I thought to myself.

An hour later I decided to go down to visit with the officer who originally told me I was assigned to Quartermaster School. When I asked what happened he told me that apparently all the seats for the next class were already filled, so I was the odd man out. He told me that the best thing to do was to report to my ship and every month or two put in a request to be released temporarily to go to the school, since it was also located in Newport. I suspected that that would be a long shot, so I asked him if he could give me a new assignment altogether. He looked up at me, pointed to the door, and said, simply, "Get the hell outta here." Which I did.

After eight weeks of enduring constant stress and harassment I finally graduated from boot camp as a seaman recruit. The day after graduation I caught a train from Chicago to Cincinnati, where I spent two weeks back home, visiting with family and friends, all the time dimly coming to realize that the familiar parts of my old neighborhood were fading into the past and my previous life was gone forever, not only because things were changing there, but because I too was now a different person than I was two months before. No longer would I roam the streets of South Fairmount seeking carefree experiences in a life where tomorrow never comes. Now life was serious, and tomorrow was something one had to plan for.

When it was time to leave home I boarded a train at the Union Terminal that took me to Washington, D. C. Then I hopped a Greyhound bus to Norfolk, Virginia, where I caught up with the USS Severn, which I boarded in late September 1959, along with another seaman apprentice I met on the bus by the name of Grady Hope. Grady was a frail, sensitive farm boy from South Carolina, entirely out of his element. We were both now 18 years old and had never been to sea before. In fact, neither of us had ever seen the sea. At first we were concerned about how we would be treated by the more experienced crew members, but they accepted us without shunning or hazing us, and we settled into our new home rather easily. In fact, within a few weeks Grady soon became a favorite of the deck force crew, perhaps because they recognized that his innocence and sincerity was both genuine and admirable.

Captain of the Head

On our second day Grady and I met with Boatswain First-Class Anderson, a sinewy old salt who had a hacking cough because he smoked cigarettes incessantly, and on his right hand he had ugly orange-brown burn stains between his forefinger and middle finger to prove it. "Boats," as we called him, had four stripes on the forearm of his uniform, indicating he had already served in the Navy for sixteen years. That meant he had signed up around 1943 to fight in World War II.

Boats told us that, as newcomers, one of us had to spend four months in the galley as a cook's assistant, and the other was to be assigned to clean the showers and toilets of the forward compartment. The cook's assistant had to rise at 4 a.m. to go back to the galley located at the rear of the ship and remain there most of the day. I didn't want to get up at 4 a.m. and go aft out into the rain and cold weather to the mess hall, where I would help make breakfast (and, later, lunch and dinner) for the crew of 300 men.

On the other hand, Grady didn't favor cleaning toilets, so we struck a deal: Grady would be the cook's assistant, and I would become "Captain of the Head" for the 50 or so crew members in our forward compartment.

Over the next few months, I daily cleaned six toilets, wash basins, mirrors and showers. This job had to be completed each day by 11 a.m., when the Executive Officer would come by and inspect my work.

The Executive Officer, who was second in command of the ship, was Commander Brown, who apparently identified with, and modelled himself after, General Douglas MacArthur. Much like his role model, Commander Brown would appear on the bridge wearing aviator sunglasses and smoking a pipe, and he issued orders in the arrogant, stone-cold voice of a condescending disciplinarian.

He had a small dog, a little poodle, that he confined to his cabin for most days, but every now and then at sea he would bring the dog onto the bridge. He would pick out a lowly deck hand who was on watch and have him hold the dog for the whole time he was on the bridge, often for two or three hours. One time the dog urinated on the deck hand while he was holding him, but Commander Brown would not allow him to set the dog down and go get cleaned up. It was at least a half-hour before the commander left the bridge and took the dog with him. The deck hand, whose shirt and undershirt were soaked in urine, was relieved from his watch and sent below by a sympathetic officer of the deck to shower and change into a new uniform.

Commander Brown reminded me of Captain Bligh from *Mutiny on the Bounty*. All the men despised him, and now and then you could hear someone whisper that if he ever came upon Commander Brown in a dark alley while ashore, the commander's next port of call would be a hospital, and I knew at least two or three of these sailors who were certainly itching to do him harm, even at the risk of a Court Martial and time in the brig. That's how much they hated him. But, as far as I know, none of them ever acted out their hidden desires.

You might think my job as Captain of the Head was the lowest job of the lowest class of sailors aboard ship, and you might be right. Here I was, four months out of high school, now 18 years old and in the Navy, literally cleaning out the shithouse every day, dumping cleanser down the commodes and scouring them with the toilet brush, removing pubic hair that collected in the shower drains, mopping up urine and, on occasion, vomit from the deck. It was not a lot of fun, I can tell you, but then I never had to go outside in bad weather and chip paint and swab the decks like the other deck force members did.

My former job at Brighton Furniture during high school had prepared me well for this detail. Not once was I ever criticized for my work. In fact, one day in a rare moment during which he actually recognized me, Commander Brown, after inspecting the sinks and commodes, told me that I was a good man for this job. I didn't know whether to feel complimented or insulted.

Our ship had recently undergone reconditioning in Norfolk, and just a few days after Grady and I came aboard the ship set sail on a "shakedown cruise" to ensure all systems were working properly. Finally, I was at sea! We headed south to the Caribbean, and a few days later my first foreign port of call was the Navy base at Guantanamo Bay, Cuba. Just a few months earlier Fidel Castro had led a successful revolution against the Batista regime, and we were warned not to leave the base, because our presence outside the base had been outlawed by the new Cuban government. All I remember of the place were the barbed-wire fences surrounding the base and Marines with rifles in the guard towers, images I recalled some thirty years later while watching the movie, *A Few Good Men*.

After a day or two in Guantanamo we weighed anchor and headed back out to sea. Our next port of call was Port-au-Prince, Haiti. The first day there I took a tour of a rum factory high in the hills, and I tasted maybe ten different varieties of rum and fruit drinks. I got so drunk I could hardly stand up. The only other thing I remember about Port-au-Prince was how much poverty there was and how horrible the living conditions were. It remains the most depressing city I have ever visited.

Two weeks later we were back at our home port in Newport, Rhode Island, which was also the location of the Quartermaster School. Almost every two weeks for the next few months I put in a chit requesting that I be allowed to take leave from the ship to attend the school, and each time I was turned down. The excuse was that I was needed aboard ship, especially now, since we would be leaving for a cruise to the North Sea to fuel ships operating there, with stops in Grenloch, Scotland and Hamburg, Germany. Somebody had to clean those commodes, and that somebody would be me. I began to have doubts about ever attending Quartermaster School.

It was in the North Sea that one of the funniest events of my time in the service took place. I was still the Captain of the Head, and daily had to deal with problems that made my work more difficult. For example, one of the ship's engineers who had the mid-watch (midnight to 4 a.m.), was allowed to sleep in until about 9 am, and he would then come to the head to wash up and relieve himself. As he sat on the commode he would take ten or fifteen minutes to read paperback cowboy novels—"shit-kickers," we called them. It was quite unpleasant to work around him, and I resented him highly for taking up so much space and interfering with my work, since I had to be ready for the Commander's inspection at 11 a.m.

One morning that November we were sailing in rough seas off the coast of Iceland. Even though the seas were turbulent and it was very cold outside, I had opened one of the forward portholes in the head to capture the breeze and collect fresh air into the compartment. The engineer was sitting there, his pants down around his ankles, reading his novel. A metal wall separated the sides of each of the commodes, but there were no doors on them.

Suddenly we hit a large wave, so large that it swamped the bow and forward deck. Before I could react, a powerful blast of sea water spurted through the porthole and totally drenched the engineer sitting on the commode. Although I realized that I had more work to do now to clean up all that salt water, I had to laugh as the engineer sat there without moving for about 20 seconds, muttering a stream of curse words as the paperback novel, now sopping wet, disintegrated in his hands and fell to the floor. There *is* justice in the universe after all, I thought as I stood there, hiding my smile while watching this poor wretch get up and leave. He never brought another novel into the head again.

A few days later we sailed up the Elbe River in northern Germany for liberty in Hamburg. I walked the streets of Hamburg and listened to the German language being spoken, and I realized that I was the first member of my family to return to our ancestral home of Germany. Little did I know then that my family's roots were located only a hundred miles or so south of Hamburg, yet it would be another forty years before I would return to Germany and visit the home of my forefathers in the city of Osnabrück.

On The Bridge

After returning to Newport that December we began to hear rumors that our ship was to be sent to the Mediterranean Sea for six months sometime in late 1960. I continued to request to go to Quartermaster School, and finally, on August 1, 1960, I was released to go, partly because our ship would not be going to sea for two months while we prepared for our Mediterranean cruise. The class lasted only five weeks, but I learned much during the time I was there. I learned about celestial navigation, keeping the ship's log, plotting courses on sea charts, being a helmsman, practicing semaphore, and memorizing Morse Code for signaling with lights.

Most importantly, upon graduation I received the designation of QMSN (Quartermaster Seaman), which meant that when I returned to my ship I would no longer be a member of the deck force, and no longer Captain of the Head. From now on I would be a member of the Communications Department, and my duty station would be on the bridge, the operational nerve center of the ship. Reporting back aboard the ship I was proud and happy that I had persisted in putting in those requests month after month. My actions had paid off, and now things indeed were looking up!

In late September 1960 we set sail from Newport for the Mediterranean Sea. The weather was pleasant for most of the trip, which would take about two weeks. One day when we were about 700 miles out in the middle of the Atlantic Ocean, the Captain cut the engines and the ship floated to a stop. The Captain then granted an hour's break for those who wanted to go swimming. At first, I resisted, but then I thought that this might be the only chance I'd ever have to do this, so I decided to test the waters. Before we were to jump in, however, a lifeboat with a rifleman was lowered over the side to protect us against any sharks that might be out looking for lunch.

I had second thoughts when I saw this, but I decided to jump in anyway. After a thirty-foot fall, I splashed into the ocean and sunk a good ten feet below the waves. I felt very alone and vulnerable for a second or two, but I didn't struggle, trusting the buoyant saltwater to boost me back up to the surface. About forty or fifty guys had jumped into the ocean, so there was a lot of slapping around of water and exuberant shouts. Everyone was having fun, swimmers and spectators alike. After swimming around for a few minutes I started to get cold, so I clambered up the cargo net to get back aboard ship.

While I dried myself off and looked down on the others who were still in the water, an image flashed through my mind. Suddenly I thought of all the people over the centuries who had drowned at sea and whose remains were at the bottom of this ocean, maybe just below us. Fifty years later I discovered in my genealogy research that my paternal great-great-grandfather, Bernard Wissing, and three of his infant children died at sea during their passage from Germany to America in 1853. As was the case in those days, the dead were wrapped in cloth and lowered over the side into their murky graves. Could it be that my ancestors' remains had rested somewhere beneath where I had been swimming?

The Mediterranean Sea

After nearly two weeks on the Atlantic Ocean, we passed through the Straits of Gibraltar and into the Mediterranean Sea. Our first port of call was Palermo, Sicily. I spent an afternoon in that hot and dusty city, which was teeming with life. Some of us took a short bus tour and ended up in the catacombs, where our guide proudly revealed to us the skeletal remains of thousands of monks. But the catacombs smelled of death and decay, and were far too dank and claustrophobic, and I couldn't wait to leave.

Back at sea I quickly and happily adapted to my new assignment as a quartermaster, standing watch on the bridge, taking my turn at the helm, keeping the ship's log, practicing celestial navigation, and plotting the ships progress on the navigational charts. We fueled many of the combat ships, from destroyers to cruisers to large aircraft carriers.

At sea, 1960.

Then one day in November 1960 I received orders that I was to transfer from the Severn to a new ship, the U.S.S. Mississinewa (AO-144), another oiler, which was homeported in Naples, Italy. Apparently one of my fellow quartermasters had volunteered for the transfer but was turned down because he had recently gone AWOL. So, I was chosen by the Navy to replace him. I was immediately depressed, since what this transfer meant was that I wouldn't be returning to America in a few months with my Severn shipmates; rather, I would be spending at least another year more in the Mediterranean. But even this chance event, which at first seemed to be bad luck, turned out to be a blessing in disguise.

What I didn't realize then was that the Mississinewa was the Flagship of the Service Force of the Sixth Fleet and had an Admiral aboard. What that meant was that we would get to visit the best ports in the Mediterranean. In addition, I soon passed my tests to become a Quartermaster Third Class (equal to a corporal in the Army) and began to move up the chain of command. Within a few months I was assigned to be the assistant to the ship's navigator, Lt. John Leaver, who became my mentor for the next 18 months.

U.S.S. Mississinewa (AO-144).

Lt. Leaver was a model officer, and I was indeed lucky to have served under him. A graduate of Dartmouth, he was about 28 years old, and had committed himself to a career in the Navy. He approached his work as the ship's navigator with a grim seriousness, although one could tell that it was also his joy. Every evening at sea we would meet in the chart room and plot the ship's position and course. He would scan the charts meticulously, pointing out hazards we wanted to avoid, or landfalls that ought to appear the following day.

While he maintained the traditional psychological distance between an officer and an enlisted man, now and then we might share a little joke, and he would turn to me with just a hint of a grin, but with a sparkle in his eyes that revealed his acceptance and validation of me. During those days he was like an older brother to me, and we worked well together.

In the Spring of 1962 we left Naples for our voyage back to the States. We were standing on the bridge steaming westward, heading towards Gibraltar and the Atlantic Ocean beyond, when Lt. Leaver suddenly stood next to me. In a moment of personal conversation he told me that he could get me assigned to a college if I stayed in the Navy, and once I graduated I would become an officer. At first I was surprised that he was talking to me like I was a regular person, which made me feel good, of course. Then I considered his offer for a moment or two.

"What will I have to commit to after college?" I asked.

"Probably another four or five years," he said.

The ship's wake grew longer and wider as Naples and Vesuvius gradually grew smaller and smaller, fading in the east behind us. I thought for a moment or two, then replied, "Thanks for the offer," I said, "but I'd rather take my chances as a civilian."

He smiled when I said that, then added, "Well, whatever you do, make sure you go to college and graduate. You can do it," he said, and that expression of support buoyed my confidence. I'll never forget his influence on me.

About ten years ago I decided to search up Lt. Leaver on the internet. I wanted to contact him and tell him that I not only graduated from college, but that I achieved an M.A. degree and a Ph.D. as well. I'm sure he would have been happy to hear that. Unfortunately, I was shocked to discover that in 1972, while he was a Commander serving as an Operations Officer on the staff of a Rear-Admiral, his helicopter was shot down in Vietnam and plummeted into the sea, and both he and the admiral were lost. That happened only ten years after I last said good-bye to him, and even though I received this news forty years later, I was nevertheless heartbroken by it.

Awakening to Life

I'm a late bloomer. Everything in my life developed later than it did in the lives of others, or so it seemed. I often thought I was three years or so behind everybody else. For example, I really didn't begin to understand about how life worked until I joined the Navy. It was there that my consciousness bloomed, and I became aware that there are choices to be made in life, and one is responsible for the consequences of those choices.

Despite my negative feelings in boot camp, I slowly began to realize that joining the Navy was not a mistake; rather, it was an experience that would benefit me. For the first time in my life I was living away from home, and away from my country. It was then that I became aware of how other people lived in different countries, seeing their customs and listening to their various languages.

By the time I was discharged from the Navy I had travelled half-way around the world and had seen many of its wonders. I had visited St. Peter's Basilica in Rome, The Haj Sophia in Istanbul, the catacombs in Palermo, the Acropolis in Athens, the Leaning Tower of Pisa, Brunelleschi's Dome in Florence, the bullrings of Valencia, the Coliseum in Rome, the French Riviera, and the island of Majorca. I had walked the streets of Istanbul, Beirut, Athens, Rome, Nice, Barcelona, Hamburg, Genoa, Palermo, Cannes and Naples. I had seen the people, heard their languages, and watched how they lived and worked. I came to realize that all these cultures and languages were equally as important as mine. And perhaps the greatest lesson I learned is that people are the same all over the world. They just do things differently.

As the leading Quartermaster I was called upon to take the helm of the ship when we passed through dangerous seas. I was only nineteen when I steered my ship through the hazardous straits of Messina, through the perilous straits of Bonifacio, through the Dardanelles, and Gibraltar—what the ancients referred to as "The Pillars of Hercules."

I also took the helm often when we fueled other ships that came alongside. And one day I stood at the helm for hours, struggling to steer the bow of the ship straight into the mountainous waves generated by hurricane-force winds. The ship shuddered as it was swamped by each on-rushing wave, and I feared that the next one, or else the one after, would finally tear the ship to pieces. It was the most terrifying day at sea I ever experienced, and the primary reason I have no desire to return. The sea is beautiful at times, but you don't want to be there when it's angry. There is no passion in the sea's embrace, just a cold and murky death.

I was also in charge of the ship's charts, and I plotted our passages to various ports throughout the Mediterranean and across the Atlantic Ocean. While on watch on the bridge I kept the ship's log, where it was my responsibility to record the minute-by-minute course changes and officer's commands. This is where I learned how to write clearly. That was important because the log was the official record of the ship's progress through the day. Here is part of an entry that I wrote in the ship's log at midnight (0000) on March 20, 1961:

> Latitude: 34 degrees, 32 minutes North
>
> Longitude: 33 degrees, 11 minutes East
>
> Steaming independently en-route to Famagusta Bay, Cyprus (ETA 0800) in accordance with CTF 63's Operation Order 52-61. On base course of 070 degrees. Speed 11 knots. #1 and #2 boilers and #1 and #2 generators are on the line. Engineering and ordinance security patrols are making hourly inspections of all lower deck spaces. Present draft is 30 feet forward, 32 feet aft.

Obviously, the language was technical and emotionless. On the other hand, that same night I wrote these remarks in my personal log:

> The midnight watch has taken over the duty. All hands are turned in except for the watch, and the bridge is the only active part of the ship. All is quiet here, except when the silence is broken by the Officer of the Deck as he orders the helmsman to change course.
>
> We are now nine miles off the southern coast of Cyprus, and the small twinkling lights of the villages that dot the shore are welcomed sights. In the eastern sky there are quick flashes of lightning now and then, followed by the dull rumble of thunder. The threat of rain may prove to have a negative effect on tomorrow's liberty in Famagusta Bay, but the men's spirits seem not to be dampened by the weather, and anticipation is running high for going ashore after ten days at sea.

Time

Just a few months after being transferred to the Mississinewa I became the leading Quartermaster. In that position I had a number of duties, and one of them was to monitor and wind the ship's chronometers, which were matched to a daily radio signal indicating the precise Greenwich Mean Time (GMT). The chronometers were probably the most important pieces of equipment aboard since they were necessary for accurate navigation.

For centuries mariners could determine their latitude (north/south) by measuring the azimuth, or angle of the sun off the horizon, but longitude (east/west) required a knowledge of the accurate time at a specific point. Christopher Columbus, and all the ancient mariners before him, knew how to figure out their latitude, but they had little idea of how to determine their longitude, except for "dead reckoning"—that is, how far they had come in the past twenty-four hours by estimating how fast the ship was going and how the current and winds might have affected it. This is why Columbus' voyage to the New World was fraught with peril. He simply had no idea where they would end up. He believed he was going to India, which is why he named the natives he found on the Caribbean Islands "Indians," a misnomer which unfortunately continues to exist.

The technology for determining longitude was not available until 1773, when an English clockmaker named John Harrison developed a marine chronometer that could be taken aboard ships and would keep relatively precise time, a time matched to the time of the principal clock of the observatory in Greenwich, England, which was located at zero longitude. The time there is now known as *Greenwich Mean Time*. By taking the angle of the evening stars with their sextants and applying that information to the exact time, mariners could now plot the ship's longitude with a considerable amount of assurance that they would be correct.

Every time our ship passed from one time zone to another it was my job, in those days before digital timekeeping, to go throughout the ship and re-wind, re-set and synchronize about 50 clocks, so our sea-going community of about 300 men would all know the proper time in this particular time zone. This was very important, since the ship's operation at sea depended upon it: reville, meals, posting of the watch, work details, etc.

While this might appear to be a dull and tedious job (and at times it was), I nevertheless got to know every part of that ship from the Captain's Cabin down to the netherworld of the engine room. And I got to meet and know the men who inhabited these spaces, from the Captain of the ship on down to the lowliest seaman—including that man who was now the Captain of the Head. I can safely say that for the period of about 18 months when I performed this duty I knew that ship inside and out better than any other man aboard, officers included.

Much of my knowledge of celestial navigation was taught to me on the Severn by my early mentor, Chief Quartermaster Burns, who showed me how to use the sextant to "shoot the stars." Chief Burns was a crusty old sailor who had joined the Navy just before WWII, and he was at Pearl Harbor when the Japanese attacked in December 1941, although he wouldn't talk much about it. He taught me to recognize important stars such as Spica, Vega, and Arcturus—placing me in the tradition that stretched all the way back to the ancient sailors who first ventured out to sea.

"Learn this now," Chief Burns said, "because in twenty years they won't be teaching it anymore."

He was right, for by 1978 the United States had developed and put into space a new Global Positioning System, Navstar, and the old days of celestial observation were coming to an end. Yet I'm glad that I learned how to rely on the sun and interpret the stars. Although I've forgotten much of what I learned then, I can still spot the brightest star north of the equator, Arcturus, in the evening sky.

So there I was at 19, a helmsman and assistant navigator on a large Navy ship sailing the Mediterranean Sea. This was the same wine-dark sea of Homer's *Odyssey*, the sea of the great naval battles of the ancient and modern worlds, the sea that delivered Columbus into the western unknown, the sea that was the very cradle of Western Civilization itself. Chance and choice had brought me to this place, and I now realize that I was extremely lucky to have had the opportunity to experience it at such a young and impressionable age.

I recall many wondrous nights, sailing with a gentle wind at our backs, the sea like a sheet of glass, with barely a ripple in it. A smooth sea soothes a sailor's soul. Often, after having shot the stars and charted our location, I would go up onto the ship's top signal deck and lie down amidships and looked up at the stars. Almost imperceptibly the ship silently swayed sideways slowly back and forth on the axis of the keel, a few degrees from port to starboard and back again, causing the stars to sway in the opposite direction of the tilt. The only sound was the gentle hiss from the spray as the ship's prow sliced through the water like scissors through cloth. The cosmos showered down its beauty upon me, and I felt at one with the universe.

WHAT THE MOON SAID

I saw the face of God in the full moon
reflected on the phosphorescent sea,
slick and sheer, off the coast of Sicily.

All was silent at midnight. The ship slept
as I stood watch. Then that shimmering face
spoke to me—and I strained my mind to listen.

And then I thought that what the moon had said
was that life's secrets lie in those questions
that men have not yet even thought to ask.

We sailed on silently towards Sicily,
The moon, the sky, the ship, the sea, and me
alone who heard that silent voice of God.

19

AS LUCK WOULD HAVE IT

*You never know what worse luck
your bad luck has saved you from.*

~ Cormac McCarthy

I should be dead. Blame it on me. It was my fault. Yet, as luck would have it, I'm still alive.

I was on my final leave to Cincinnati in April 1962, just short of my 21st birthday and less than two months before my discharge from the Navy. It was about three in the morning as I headed home from my date, driving my sister Roseann's brand new 1962 Comet down Winton Road. I was drowsy because I'd been up so late, and I rolled the window down now and then to stick my head out into the cold rushing air to stay awake. But the technique didn't work, and I fell asleep at the wheel and crashed, hitting a wooden telephone pole and severing it.

Just before the crash I awoke when the car bounced over the curb and I instinctively hit the brakes, and in very slow motion I saw what was happening, but it was too late to avoid the inevitable. These were the days before airbags, and I wasn't wearing a seat belt. My head hit the steering wheel hard and almost knocked me out. Stunned, I looked up I saw that the top of the severed telephone pole had swung out on its wires and then swung back like a pendulum, smashing into the Comet's roof and windshield, coming to rest no more than six inches from my head, almost crushing my skull. That's how close I came to death.

Barely conscious, I step out of the car and staggered around it, cursing my stupidity and bad luck. The car was a total wreck, and I wondered how I was going to tell my sister. Just then I saw that the front wheel on the passenger's side was hanging over a thirty-foot embankment, spinning slowly to a stop. The bottom of the telephone pole was still in the ground, and that had prevented the car from moving forward.

Had I not struck the pole, there would have been nothing to keep the car from flipping over the embankment and rolling over and over down into a deep ravine. I surely would not have survived that, and even if I did I would not have been found for hours, since there were no other cars on the road that early in the morning, and no one had witnessed the accident.

And I'm certain that had I gone over that embankment and rolled down into the ravine I wouldn't be here in my old age writing about my automobile crash when I was just twenty years old. You wouldn't be reading this story, and my two sons and my grandchildren would never have been born. This event revealed to me how chance, or luck, can play a significant role in one's life. It was my bad luck to hit that telephone pole. Yet, as luck would have it, that pole undoubtedly saved me from even worse luck: death itself.

20

COLLEGE DAYS

Live as if you will die tomorrow.
Learn as if you were to live forever.

~ Gandhi

I was discharged from the Navy just before my 21st birthday. By that time I had traveled halfway around the world and visited many countries that few my age had ever seen, or ever will. These experiences provided me with a consciousness and a world view that I never had before, and I returned home to Cincinnati with a new self-confidence and a desire to fulfill the promise I had made to myself that first day in boot camp three years earlier—to go to college.

I had been able to wrangle an early discharge in May of 1962 so I could begin summer school session at Xavier University in Cincinnati, which had already accepted me. My appeal for an early discharge was based on the fact that our ship was to be dry-docked in the shipyards in Hoboken, New Jersey for six months of reconditioning. But, as a quartermaster, my duties as a helmsman and assistant navigator were no longer required. So, just two months shy of my 21st birthday I was given an honorable discharge. I had spent two years and 11 months in the Navy, but I was given credit for four years of service.

During my time at sea I had saved up enough money to pay for my first year or so of college. How I would finance the next three years I didn't know, but I didn't hesitate to sign up for my courses and begin my studies. Since algebra had been my most difficult subject in high school, and since there was a math requirement at Xavier, I decided to sign up for the basic algebra course. It was the only class I signed up for that summer session, and I thought if I could put all my attention on passing algebra (recalling my stressful high school classes with Father Aldric), everything else in college would be a breeze. So that's what I did, and somehow I passed the algebra course, and everything else did prove to be much easier.

That fall I declared myself an English major, since it was the only subject I felt confident in, and one of the few majors that interested me. I also began to get involved in extra-curricular activities, such as writing an arts and entertainment column for the student newspaper and participating in speech contests. At the same time, to meet my expenses, I began working twenty hours a week in the cashier's office at the Coca-Cola plant conveniently located on Dana Avenue, directly across the street from Xavier's South Hall.

I ran out of the money I'd saved in the Navy by the middle of my sophomore year, so I went to the Dean of Students to appeal for a loan to finance my future studies. The dean denied my request for a loan in one breath, but in the next he told me that he was going to appoint me a "Dean's Scholar," and for the next 2½ years I would go to school free—so long as I maintained good grades and continued to participate in the life of the university.

It was a stroke of good fortune. I don't know why the Dean did this, but I was very grateful, and I continued to apply myself to my studies and extra-curricular activities. I began acting in theater with the Masque Society, became editor of *Xavier News* in 1964-65, and did well enough in my courses that I was appointed a member of Alpha Sigma Nu, the National Jesuit Honor Society for academic excellence.

Carolyn O'Donnell and I were married on August 28, 1965, in the Bellarmine Chapel at Xavier University. My high-school sweetheart, Carolyn had recently graduated from Mount St. Joseph's College in Cincinnati, and I was beginning my senior year at Xavier. By the time I graduated in May of 1966 Carolyn was pregnant with our first child, Richard Dylan, who was born on August 1, 1966. I was watching TV in the hospital waiting room when the nurse came out and congratulated me on the birth of our son. That happy moment was somewhat tempered by the sad news report I had just been watching on TV—it was the day of the Texas Tower mass shooting.

By the spring of 1966 I had been accepted to three university graduate programs. Notre Dame offered me a four-year course of study leading to a Ph.D. in English, and the University of Maryland had done the same. But I decided that I didn't want to continue on in the field of English, so I took the third offer, a two-year Master of Arts program in American Studies at Purdue University.

It was while at Purdue that I began to realize, ever so dimly, that I had developed, since as early as grade school, a love for learning. It was not a love motivated by thoughts of a career filled with future wealth and riches; rather, it was a hunger for learning for its own sake, a hunger not simply for knowledge itself, but a hunger for understanding. And that hunger cultivated in me positive feelings that this was what I was meant to be in life—a scholar.

The following two years we spent living in West Lafayette, Indiana. I took graduate courses in American history, sociology, economics, philosophy and English at Purdue. American Studies was a new field of inquiry, and I was happy that I was exposed to such a wide variety of courses that would allow me to integrate them into a better understanding of the American experience. The first year I spent as a teaching assistant in the English department, teaching basic composition.

In the summer of the second year I got a job writing newsletters and brochures for The Committee on Institutional Cooperation (CIC), a consortium of the Big Ten Colleges that had its main office on the Purdue campus. The income from that job, more than double that of what I had received as a teaching assistant, was very helpful and necessary, for during that summer Carolyn became pregnant with our second son, James Cullen, who was born on February 24, 1968.

The Purdue years were full of stress for us. My classes and my job gave me little time for family, and Carolyn grew depressed, especially after her second pregnancy. I was able to get her into classes in the English Department, however, and that made her much happier. I was also uneasy about what I would do once I received my M.A. in American Studies. For one thing, I had spent too much time in library, and my eyesight had suffered from reading so much that I had to buy glasses.

It was during this time I became very disappointed with the Catholic Church, since we had been practicing "The Rhythm Method," the only kind of natural contraception permitted by the Church. But after two pregnancies in three years, it obviously wasn't working for us. Then one day Carolyn came home to report that the priest in the Catholic Newman Center on campus was advising women in the confessional to use condoms or other forms of birth control that were officially outlawed by the Church. I couldn't believe it, for here was a priest telling us that what the pope in Rome said about birth control was wrong. I began thinking to myself, who's in charge of this Church?

A few weeks later Carolyn and her sister Cathy went to Chicago on the weekend to tour colleges that Cathy was considering attending, and that Sunday morning I was home alone with our infant son, Richard Dylan. I decided then and there that I would not get up and go to Mass, and that I no longer wanted to be a member of the Catholic Church. It was raining outside, and as I lay in bed I thought for sure that God would send a lightning bolt down to strike me dead and I would go to Hell for all eternity!

Yet, there were no lightning strikes, and when I awoke I was not in Hell. But I was finished with religion. Once I made that decision all the dominoes began to fall, and all my old standards and values came into question. I abandoned many of them, but I also began to adopt new values to replace the old ones. My apostasy was a difficult but important step, one that helped liberate me from my past life, a life that had kept me in the chains of traditions that had inhibited me from realizing who I was and who I wanted to become.

During the winter of 1967 I entered my final year of studies at Purdue. I didn't know what I was going to do once I received my M.A. the following Spring, although my boss at the CIC had secured me a scholarship to the University of Michigan towards a Ph.D. in Education. I was flattered by the offer, but I wasn't really interested in the field of Education.

Next to our apartment in West Lafayette was an open cornfield, and I took a walk through the field one brisk evening in October 1967, contemplating what to do next. After mulling over my options, I decided to turn to a future in the arts and apply to Ohio State University's Ph.D. program in Theater. I had no idea it was going to work, but it was one of those decisive moments when I made a choice that would thrust my life into an entirely new direction. Then one morning about two months after I applied, I received a letter in the mail informing me that not only had I been accepted into the Ph.D. program, but I also had won a two-year academic fellowship in the Theatre Department at Ohio State beginning in the Fall of 1968, all expenses paid, along with a monthly stipend of $300.

America was in social turmoil in the summer of 1968. The Vietnam War dragged on with no end in sight. Both Martin Luther King and Bobby Kennedy had just been assassinated. Cities were on fire as a result of civil rights protests. The Democratic Convention in Chicago that August was chaotic, as left-wing protestors were beaten in the streets by Mayor Daley's police. A new counterculture was evolving in America, one that questioned the traditional values of society and demanded change. Over the next two years college campuses raged with anti-war and civil rights protests that reached their peak on May 4, 1970, with the killing of four college students at Kent State University by the Ohio National Guard. These were intense times indeed.

In September 1968 we settled into our rental home in Columbus, Ohio. We were virtually penniless, but I was able to secure Carolyn a teaching assistantship, and she was also accepted into the M.F.A. program in the Theater Department. Our meager monthly salaries were supplemented by a national Vietnam Era Veterans Benefits Program stipend of $300 a month that I received as a result of my service in the Navy. Together we were earning almost a thousand dollars a month. In those days it was enough to get by, but there was very little left by the end of the month. We were living paycheck to paycheck, and obviously had no money in a savings account.

But we were still in our twenties, and the arts, especially theater, were flourishing. Many of us involved in theater believed we were going to change the world, and in a number of ways we did, although, as it turned out, not as much as we thought we would. Experimental theater troupes such as The Living Theatre and Grotowski's Poor Theatre were springing up around the country. Mime also became popular. The musicals "Hair" and "Jesus Christ Superstar" were introducing counter-culture ideas into mainstream society, and films like *Easy Rider* were doing the same.

I was happily taking courses in theater history and production, and I also began taking courses in photography and film, which became my minor field of study. I was more than satisfied that I made the decision to attend Ohio State, and I began to commit myself, and the rest of my life, to the arts. It was a rigorous lifestyle we were living, what with classes, scholarship, theater productions, and raising two children under three years of age. But we were young, and we were enjoying it.

While all this was happening, another significant event took place that profoundly altered my way of thinking about the world and my place in it. One Friday evening in early October 1968 we were invited to a graduate student party. I only knew one or two new friends who would be there, and at first we were reluctant to go. But then we changed our minds and decided at the last minute to attend the party. That decision led to an important chance encounter.

The party was a typical graduate student affair, with strangers getting to know each other over drinks and music, and everyone trying hard to impress and act sophisticated. Not one for small talk, I typically stayed back and didn't engage too much. But after a beer or two I began to circulate, and then I found myself drawn to a group of three or four medical students who were talking about a new federally funded program in the Psychology Department, led by a rather well-known psychopharmacologist, Dr. Roland Fischer. I had no idea what psychopharmacology was, and I'd never heard of Dr. Fischer. The medical students told me that Dr. Fischer was seeking graduate student volunteers from various disciplines to test their reactions to a hallucinogenic drug called psilocybin, which was a manufactured drug chemically equivalent to the "magic mushroom." By chance I had stumbled into this conversation at exactly the right time.

Although it was 1968 and I was 27, I had never taken illegal drugs, not even marijuana. I could have walked away from that conversation then and there. But I was fascinated by what the medical students were saying, and they gave me the contact number I could call to volunteer for the program. Within two weeks I was sitting in Dr. Fischer's office taking a personality test that would indicate whether or not I would be a suitable volunteer.

Apparently I did well enough, because a week later I got a phone call inviting me to participate in the program the following Saturday morning. I was excited that I was accepted, but wary, too, since I had never participated in such an experiment before, and I was concerned about what effect the drug might have on me. Still, I decided to take a chance and see what would happen. That choice was one of the most crucial decisions I ever made. It was a decisive moment that had a profound impact on my life.

The following Saturday I walked into a conference room at the Ohio State University Hospital, where the experiment would take place. About eight other graduate students from various disciplines were there as well. A graduate assistant to Dr. Fischer took our temperature and weight, and then dispensed a cup of water and a small pill containing psilocybin to each of us, letting us know that the drug would not take effect until about twenty minutes after we swallowed it. So, we settled in around a table getting to know each other, and every now and then one or two of us would be called out of the room for tests. After ten minutes or so I was called into another room, where I took a depth/recognition test of objects presented on a screen. That was simple enough, I thought.

However, by the time I returned to the meeting room ten minutes later, things had changed. Everything and everyone appeared smooth and fluid. The edges of their personalities were rounded off, so to speak, and an air of serene pleasure permeated the room. Time also became distorted, and everything seemed to be happening in slow motion, perhaps because each event now caught my attention and caused me to pause as it revealed its significance. Obviously the drug was beginning to have an effect on me, and those around me as well. Our conversations seemed at once both profoundly wise and extremely funny. We spent much of the next hour laughing.

I began to feel euphoric, as if I had thrown off my self-consciousness, or that I had lost my ego, or rather transcended it, and that I was now part of something greater than I had ever experienced before. I walked through those "doors of perception" into an altered state of psychedelic consciousness, a land of new awareness where pretense and artificiality had faded away. It was as if a veil had been lifted from my eyes and I could see the world for what it really was. I experienced a "oneness," a harmonious sharing of being, with the people around me, with Nature outside the window, and even with nearby objects like a pencil, the hairs on the back of my wrist, or the chair I was sitting on. All those things I had normally taken for granted I now experienced in their being and their beauty for the first time in my life. I began to understand the essence, the "this-ness" of that ordinary pencil I held in my hand, and in comprehending its essence I saw its beauty, and I melded with that beauty and became one with the pencil, appreciating its being and beauty in a way I'd never encountered before.

Many who undergo such experiences often find them difficult to describe, perhaps because we haven't yet developed the proper vocabulary to describe them. I struggle to recount everything that happened, realizing only that I saw far more than I can relate. This was my experience, and only I could undergo it. It is one of those experiences that each person has to undergo for themselves. In the end, words fail to transmit the experience. All I can say is that it was then that I began to comprehend Walt Whitman's cosmic sense of being at one with the world, with Nature, with the Cosmos.

And I saw, like Whitman, that death was nothing to fear, and that the foundation of life was love, and that much of what I had been taught as a child by nuns and priests and parents and politicians and society at large was not in harmony with this new vision, and that most of my early education had little to do with learning, but more to do with socializing me to blend into the society in which I was raised. I recalled what Whitman had written: "Re-examine all you have been told at school or church or in any book, and dismiss whatever insults your own soul." Moreover—and this is the really important part—the drug gave me permission to be me, to be myself, and for the first time in my life I felt validated and authentic as a person.

There are those rare moments in life when the beauty of the universe reveals itself and an understanding of one's being and purpose is achieved. This was one of those moments for me, and its revelation of the beauty of existence stimulated my confidence and self-esteem in a way I'd never experienced before. For a brief moment I'd been given a vision, a peek into some of the secrets of the universe. As a result, I was able to shrug off many of the remnants of my past and be free to do what I wanted to do with my life, to follow my passion. I felt I had escaped from the rules and regulations of the past—at least for the moment.

I say, "at least for the moment," because when the drug wore off I lost that altered state of consciousness. As soon as I left the hospital, the rules and restrictions of daily life crept back in, nagging at me, demanding obedience, insisting that I conform to the ways of the world and what was expected of me. And this struggle remains a daily constant for me: whether to conform to the norms of society, or to liberate myself from them so I could intellectually and artistically develop the ideas and create the works that would bring meaning and satisfaction to my life. Most of the time I am able to negate conformity and affirm creativity, but even today it is not always easy going.

The psilocybin experiments lasted for about a year, and during that time I was called in every two or three months to participate. I took four or five "trips," or psychedelic adventures, all of which were legal. Every time I took the drug my consciousness and self-esteem were reinforced with assurances that my intuition about the world and my life in it were correct, and each time I came away feeling that the creative life was the life I was meant to lead.

It was as if I had shed my old life of doubt, hesitation and second-guessing, and entered a new world of creative self-reliance. I realize now that I was disenchanted with "normal life," not because I felt I was above it, or that I deserved better than that. No, it wasn't a matter of status, or class, or feelings of superiority; rather, it was a matter of determining for myself what area of life provided me the most delight, satisfaction and purpose. That area was the arts, and the arts became my passion and my reason for living.

The rest of my life would be spent pursuing the beauty of the world in various artistic ways: theater, film, photography, poetry and prose. Ultimately I was able to parlay my work in the arts into a full-time university teaching position. I taught film production, film history, screenwriting and acting. Every day at that job I took part in creative activities with my students, and every day we were involved in serious play. When I look back on it, I realize that I had a job that I loved, and that I never really worked a day in 40 years—yet all the while I got paid for it!

21

JFK'S FUNERAL

For Lycidas is dead, dead 'ere his prime....

Lycidas
~ John Milton

Like most people my age, I remember precisely where I was on the day President John Kennedy was assassinated, November 22, 1963. I'd just finished a mid-term exam in my sophomore poetry class at Xavier, where I had written, coincidentally, an essay on "Lycidas," the poem by John Milton about the untimely death of one of his young friends. As a stepped out of the classroom someone ran past me with astonishing news, "Rich, President Kennedy's been shot!" Staggered by the news, I walked to Bellarmine Chapel, knelt down in a pew and mumbled a few prayers for JFK. It was only a short time later when Walter Cronkite emotionally announced what everyone was dreading: Kennedy was dead.

That day is etched forever in my memory. But I also remember quite clearly where I was two days later: up a tree—literally. On Saturday afternoon, November 23rd, the day after the assassination, three of my Xavier classmates and I decided to pool our meager funds and drive overnight from Cincinnati to Washington, D. C. to attend JFK's funeral procession from the White House to the Capitol the next morning.

We arrived in Washington about 10 a.m., and the crowd was already eight-to-ten people deep on the sidewalks of Pennsylvania Avenue. At first I was concerned that I wouldn't be able to see anything. But then I spied a tree devoid of leaves, and I climbed up and claimed a spot that provided me with a good vantage point from which to watch the funeral procession.

Not only did I have a good view of the funeral route, but I also could see all along Pennsylvania Avenue, up towards the White House and down to the Capitol. Throngs of people lined both sides of the avenue. Estimates were that 300,000 people had come out that day to pay their respects. At twenty-two, I had never been part of such a large gathering in my life. Nor would I ever be again.

I settled into my roost and was trying to keep warm when someone just below me who had a transistor radio began to yell out, "Oswald's been shot! Oswald's been shot!" Like the effect you get when you throw a stone into a lake, the news rippled out in waves all along the route for as far as I could see. Many cheered and applauded upon hearing the news, as if some moral retribution had just taken place. But I must confess that certain sadness overwhelmed me then, for all I could repeat in my perch above it all was, "Now we'll never know. Now we'll never know."

An hour or so later the funeral passed by: the muffled drums, the caisson bearing JFK's remains, the riderless horse, and the Kennedy family. The crowd was respectfully quiet, although many openly shed tears. White handkerchiefs dotted the sea of faces. The sadness was so intense I could feel it rising from the street. It was clear that these people genuinely loved this man, and I felt I was witnessing a defining moment in 20th Century American history.

After the funeral passed I jumped down to the ground and joined my friends and hundreds of others following the procession on foot to the Capitol. Once in the crowd, I turned to find myself walking an arm's length away from Charles de Gaulle and Halie Selassie, the emperor of Ethiopia, and I was surprised to see that they, and scores of other foreign dignitaries, had no security surrounding and protecting them. Such openness, I thought, would come to an end in the years that followed.

The lines were so long outside the Capitol rotunda where JFK's body lay in state that we decided we couldn't afford to wait for hours to pay our respects. Instead, we turned around and drove for twelve hours back to Cincinnati, each of us quiet for long periods of time, silently lost in our personal grief. As we drove into the night, I thought about the country's loss, and how, for one brief shining moment, JFK brought us a fresh spirit of change and hope for a brighter tomorrow. But now Camelot was over. Hope was gone, and I felt then that America would never be the same after that day I spent up a tree in Washington, D.C., November 24, 1963.

22

LORENZO TUCKER

He's the Colored Valentino!

~ Oscar Micheaux

My final story is one based on choice and chance. I made some choices, and as I was going down one path, chance intervened, and I ended up on a different path altogether. It is a story about how chance can shape one's life–in this case, for the better.

Two things happened in 1983 that were to have a major impact on my life. I was teaching a documentary film class when I read a newspaper article about black men in Philadelphia who met on Saturday mornings to ride horses at Cobbs Creek Park. Their goal was to preserve the history of black cowboys and "Buffalo Soldiers."

After the Civil War a large number of freed black men went west and became cowboys, yet their contributions to building the West is rarely mentioned in history books. The only time you saw blacks in cowboy movies was when they played the chuck wagon cook or other menial or stereotypical comic roles. But the untold story is that they made a significant contribution to the development of the West.

"Buffalo Soldiers" were what the Native Americans called the African American soldiers who joined the U.S. Army Calvary after the Civil War and fought against the Native Americans in the Southwest. The Native Americans called them that because the black soldiers' natural hair reminded them of the hair on the hide of the buffalo.

The story intrigued me, and I decided to take my student film crew out to document these men and their activities. We made a short five-minute film about them, but I thought that there was a bigger film here, and I began to do research on the history of black cowboys.

During that time I was called into the office of my department chairman, who told me that if I didn't have my dissertation completed and my Ph.D. in hand by September 1, 1986, I wouldn't get tenure and would lose my job. I had abandoned the Ph.D. program in Theater and Film at Ohio State University in 1973 and had given up on my dissertation, partly due to my involvement in the anti-war movement at OSU, and partly because I felt I had not received any good advice from my dissertation advisor, who I believe had disowned me because of my anti-war activism.

So, a decade later, I called one of my former professors at OSU and asked if there were a way to get back into the Ph.D. program and finish my dissertation. After consulting the committee, he reported that they would let me back in; however, while I didn't have to repeat any classes, I would nevertheless be required to take my General Exams over again and complete my dissertation by August of 1986. I began work at once, although I had no idea that I would be able to finish what was a rather monumental task, and I had no idea of a topic for my dissertation.

In January 1984 I was in Los Angeles at the Academy of Motion Picture Arts and Sciences' library to do research on black cowboy films that were made in the late 1930s. I began my research by browsing through the shelves of books. There, by chance, I happened to spot a book called *Blacks in Black and White*, a collection of brief biographical sketches of black actors who had appeared in early motion pictures. Picking that book off the shelf was another event that changed the direction of my life.

I began thumbing through the book and, believe it or not, the first page I opened contained a photograph of Lorenzo Tucker, a black actor once known as "The Colored Valentino." Included was a brief, one-page summary of Tucker's film career. Intrigued, I read the sketch and found that he had been born in Philadelphia in 1907. Could it be that he might still be alive? I immediately thought that a more complete biography of this man might be an acceptable topic for my Ph.D. dissertation. My work on the black cowboy movie stopped then and there, since mere chance had led me to pick up that book and open it to the page of Lorenzo Tucker. Or was it more than mere chance?

When I returned home to New Jersey I contacted my dissertation committee with a proposal to write Tucker's biography, and they agreed to accept the topic. I then set about to see if Tucker was still alive, so I could interview him. In those days before the internet the only methods of long-distance communication were letter writing and the telephone, and my first phone call was to the *New York Times* obituary section, to see if they had any recent death notices on Tucker, who had been born in 1907 and would now be in his late 70s. There was no obituary, so I made a few more phone calls, but they led nowhere, and I was beginning to get discouraged. Yet, I had one final idea: I thought that if Lorenzo was still alive he might be living in Los Angeles. It was a long shot, but I phoned the Los Angeles White Pages, thinking that there were probably a number of pages of people named Tucker, but how many Lorenzo's would there be?

There was one.

I jotted down the number and decided to call. The phone rang two, three, four times, and I was just about ready to hang up and give up on ever finding this man and writing his story. But I decided to wait a little longer, and on about the seventh ring Lorenzo picked up the phone—he had just walked in the door and heard the phone ringing. Nervously I introduced myself and told him about my idea to write his story. He was skeptical at first, but when I told him I was not only a professor, but an actor as well, he opened up to me, and we talked for a good twenty minutes. He agreed to meet with me, so just before we hung up I told him I would arrange to come to Los Angeles to visit with him soon.

It was February 1984 when I arrived at his apartment house on Las Palmas Avenue, just a block north of Hollywood Boulevard. I buzzed his apartment number, and he came down to open the locked entrance way. We shook hands, and the first thing he said to me was, "Damn, you're as tall as I am!" At that moment I knew we would become close friends. Later I realized that this was also the moment that fate had brought me to this man, and that I had been chosen, by some strange force, to write the story of his life.

For a brief period in the late 1920s and early '30s, Lorenzo Tucker starred as a black screen idol in a dozen films, most of them "Race Movies"—films made by blacks, with all-black casts, for all-black audiences. Almost all of these films were directed by his mentor, Oscar Micheaux, who is now recognized as the most important independent black film producer/director of the first half of the twentieth century.

Over the course of the next 18 months I visited Lorenzo numerous times, recording our conversations. I would also talk with him over the phone to verify other information about him and his times, including factual details I had researched at the Schomburg Library in Harlem, and at the Library of Congress in Washington, D. C.

Lorenzo Tucker in "The Black King" (1932).

As the months rolled by the biography began to take shape. At the same time, I was studying for my General Exams, and in August I returned to Ohio State and re-took the exams: three days of writing for six hours each day, answering questions that the members of my committee had submitted to me. It was a grueling ordeal, but I passed. One of my professors who was on my original committee twelve years prior jokingly remarked, "Richard, we've had Ph.D. candidates take the exam over because they flunked it the first time, but you are the only one I know of who has taken the exam twice and passed it both times!"

Now I directed my attention solely on my work on Tucker, even though I was holding down my job as a full-time professor and raising a family as well. Most of my evening were spent in my office from 7 to 10 p.m., researching and writing. I had less than two years to complete this full-length biography, so time was of the essence. Also, I visited with Lorenzo a number of times, and each time we grew closer and closer as friends, and he became something of a father figure for me, dispensing information and advice on a number of topics.

In May 1986 I accompanied Lorenzo to the Director's Guild of America, where they were honoring Oscar Micheaux's pioneering work in black filmmaking. They were also giving him a star on Hollywood Boulevard. Micheaux had directed Lorenzo Tucker in a dozen of silent and sound films in the 1920s and '30s, and he had dubbed Tucker "The Colored Valentino."

The Master of Ceremonies for the occasion was Sidney Poitier who, when he saw Lorenzo in the audience, asked him to stand and be recognized. Poitier then called Tucker "The godfather of black actors in America." Tucker received warm applause and was truly moved by the recognition given him. Later, when Poitier left the stage he approached Lorenzo and shook his hand, Lorenzo introduced me to Sidney, saying, "This is Professor Grupenhoff. He's my official biographer!" It was indeed an honor and pleasure for me to meet such an important actor and trailblazer for African American actors in Hollywood films.

That was to be Lorenzo's final public appearance. I later came to feel that the recognition he received from Sidney Poitier at the Directors Guild was the moment when he gave into the disease that he secretly knew was destroying his body. About two weeks later while crossing the street he collapsed and was rushed to the hospital. I spoke to Lorenzo on the phone while he was in the hospital. He was in denial, telling me that it was a minor setback and that he would be up and about shortly. Later that day Lorenzo's wife, Pauline, called me to tell me the truth: Lorenzo had inoperable lung cancer, and the hospital would be sending him home to his apartment soon for his final days.

Pauline asked me to come visit him, for he had told her that he wanted to see me.

A few days later I flew to Los Angeles and went immediately to see Lorenzo. He had lost a lot of weight since I last saw him three months earlier. He was bedridden, and the situation was indeed grim. He was pleased to see me, and the first thing he asked was, "Is the book finished yet?" I'd recently completed the first draft and it was going through minor revisions, so I felt it fair to say, "Yes, it's finished."

"Good," he said, "because I don't think I'm going to beat this, and now that the book is done, I can rest easy."

"Everyone is pulling for you to make it through this," I replied, knowing my remark was a feeble one. He simply smiled. I sat next to him, holding his hand while we talked, and now and then he would nod off to sleep for a few minutes.

As I walked back to my Hollywood hotel that smoggy Los Angeles evening I found myself almost wishing him to pass away so he could be rid at last of his terrible physical pain and of the emotional embarrassment it must have caused him to be seen as a mere shadow of his former self. It was the final irony of this one-time screen lover to be dying in a small apartment on an obscure side-street of Hollywood, almost penniless and forgotten by all but a few. Yet it wasn't the first time such a story had unfolded in Hollywood, and it certainly won't be the last.

Back in my hotel room I recollected the day's events and reflected that I had been disappointed in myself for not having been more of a comfort to Lorenzo earlier that day. I decided that tomorrow I would tell him that no matter what happens his life was not lived in vain, and that his story would be an example to us all. But I was denied that opportunity, because around midnight I received a phone call from Pauline. She informed me that Lorenzo had passed away at 11:42 p.m.

Lorenzo Tucker was different from his contemporaries in many ways. He was born into a northern urban environment; the southern countryside and the plantation heritage of his ancestors was alien to him. He disliked farm life, finding his natural milieu in the excitement and energy of the big city. He was a precocious child whose light complexion enhanced his prospects for success as a black doctor or lawyer, but he found formal education restrictive, and he opted instead for the tenuous existence of an entertainer. He was a Renaissance Man during the Harlem Renaissance of the 1920s: urbane, sophisticated, dignified, intelligent, handsome, creative, full of life and the spirit of equality, and not without a few tricks of his own to guarantee his survival. His central peculiarity was his light skin, which permitted him at times a double existence—a black man who could also pass as white.

"I was too black to be white, and too white to be black," he often lamented. And, while he sometimes used his lightness to his advantage, he never denied that he was of the black race.

Lorenzo Tucker was a kind of cultural courier who moved back and forth through the black and white worlds, observing prejudice from both sides, seeing it for the evil that it was—and continues to be. His life was a struggle to eradicate that evil and be accepted for who he was in an age when blacks sought equality in vain. He wasn't always successful, but his life was rich and full of accomplishments. In the end it was the struggle for racial equality to which he remained dedicated, and although he had his faults and shortcomings, his life was a model to be emulated.

My dissertation on Tucker was accepted by the faculty at Ohio State, and on August 29, 1986 I walked in the graduation procession and received my Ph.D.—three days before the deadline for me to receive tenure at my college. Later, in March 1988, my biography of Tucker, *The Black Valentino: The Stage and Screen Career of Lorenzo Tucker*, was published. (The publisher refused to use the word "colored," insisting it was now out of fashion and inappropriate.)

With that publication, and other articles on black film history, I became one of the first film historians that began to uncover the rich history of early African American independent filmmaking. For the next thirty years I taught hundreds of university students about that subject. By doing so I was able to keep the life and times of Lorenzo Tucker alive in our collective memory. Every six months or so I dream of him and the good times we shared. When I awake I rarely remember the conversations we had in the dream, but I feel blessed for having the opportunity to visit with him once again.

That is the story of how my desire to make a film about black cowboys was interrupted by chance and circumstances and sent in an entirely new direction. Instead, I chose to write the biography of Lorenzo Tucker, a decision that changed my life and solidified my academic career. And I never made that film about black cowboys.

23

THE END GAME

> *We are such stuff as dreams are made of,*
> *and our little lives are rounded with a sleep.*
>
> Prospero, *The Tempest*
> ~ William Shakespeare

Finally, for every beginning of a story there is an end, and we have come to the point where this story ends. I've left a number of events and memories from my life out of this story because they are irrelevant. Those that might be considered relevant—but which I choose not to tell—remain my secrets, and I will take them to the grave. Whatever more there is to be said I will leave to others. I've said enough. It's time for me, as Prospero suggests, to prepare for my final sleep.

That great American movie icon and pop-philosopher, Mae West, was right, I think. She said, "You only live once, but if you do it right, once is enough." When I look back on my life, I must admit that I didn't always "do it right." Most of us who admit to our imperfections will agree that it's not always easy to do the right thing, and my experiences show that doing the wrong thing is often much easier. Still, most of the time I tried my best to do the right thing. In the long view, however, I did what I did, and I'll have to live and die with that. One simply has no other choice.

Mine has been a life of joy and sorrow, of pleasure and pain, of triumph and failure, and of desires fulfilled and unfulfilled. I don't presume to serve as a model for anyone's life but my own, and I will die knowing that, despite my many personal shortcomings, I am happy to have lived the life given to me, blessed to have seen the beauty of this world, grateful to have been loved and to have loved those I have loved, and exhilarated by the beauty and incredible experience of life itself. One can ask for little more.

As I say goodbye and depart into the cosmic swirl of the universe and join the spirits of all those billions of men and women who have gone before me, my only request is that you remember me now and again, for our thoughts and memories of those who are no longer with us contribute to our understanding and to the evolution of the universe, and that's important, for memory is the treasury and guardian of all things.

FAREWELL

I dreamed my dream, and to me it seemed
as if this world, despite its strife,
was a fine place to live my life
as best I could
not as I should
but as I would.

EPILOGUE

*How green was my valley then,
and the valley of them that have gone.*

How Green was My Valley
~ Richard Llewellyn

All is gone now. Lost to time is that once green and vibrant South Fairmount valley that nurtured generations. Lost, too, are my parents, who loved me more than I knew. Lost are all those neighbors who waved to me as I delivered their newspapers. Gone are the days I spent with my friends, roaming the streets of South Fairmount, carefree, believing that tomorrow would never come.

Gone is that beautiful church and school of Saint Bonnies, my second home when I was just a kid. Gone, too, are the nuns and priests who taught me well and prepared me for my future. Gone is the altar, the stained-glass windows, the statues, the candles, the choir and their songs. Never again will Saint Bonnies' bells echo down through the valley, and never again will the church doors swing open to celebrate Midnight Mass on Christmas Eve, or the resurrection of Christ on Easter Sunday. There will be no more baptisms, no more weddings, and no more funerals of the faithful. All that is gone.

Lost also to the past is Shadwell Park, where we swam on warm summer afternoons, and played baseball until the sun set. Gone is the West Hills Theater, Niehoff's Dairy, Spring Garden Bank, Queen Anne's Confectionary and Firehouse #21. All those places are gone forever, as are all those shops and homes where people lived in those days when this valley was green with life and laughter and love, and full of grace.

All those people and places are now gone forever, lost to time. Yet, while they are gone from our sight, they still live in our hearts, and we carry them with us wherever we go. They will remain alive in our thoughts and memories, and they will never die until we die and join them in that next green valley, which lies just over that final hill we all must climb, each in our own time.

ABOUT THE AUTHOR

Dr. Richard L. Grupenhoff is a Professor Emeritus of Rowan University in Glassboro, New Jersey, where he spent 40 years teaching everything film related.

He is the author of *The Black Valentino: the Stage and Screen Career of Lorenzo Tucker,* and is recognized for his pioneering scholarship of Independent African American film production, particularly the "race movies" of the 1920s and '30s.

Other titles include *Fool's Gold*, a CD compilation of poetry.

A former actor, he has also written and directed several stage plays and films.

Richard was born and raised in the South Fairmount neighborhood of Cincinnati, Ohio. After serving in the Navy, he attended Xavier University and then Ohio State University, where he earned his Ph.D. in Theater and Film.

He now lives in Southern New Jersey, in a suburb of Philadelphia, PA.

When he's not playing Senior Softball, he's spending time in his lakeside geodesic dome with his life partner, Carol Ann DeSimine.

www.ingramcontent.com/pod-product-compliance
Lightning Source LLC
LaVergne TN
LVHW051048080426
835508LV00019B/1771